English History Stories

50 True and Fascinating Tales of Major Events and People from England's Past

Welcome Aboard, Check Out This Limited-Time Free Bonus!

Ahoy, reader! Welcome to the Ahoy Publications family, and thanks for snagging a copy of this book! Since you've chosen to join us on this journey, we'd like to offer you something special.

Check out the link below for a FREE e-book filled with delightful facts about American History.

But that's not all - you'll also have access to our exclusive email list with even more free e-books and insider knowledge. Well, what are ye waiting for? Click the link below to join and set sail toward exciting adventures in American History.

Access your bonus here
https://ahoypublications.com/
Or, Scan the QR code!

Table of Contents

Introduction

History is a fascinating adventure with exciting stories, inspirational people, and decisive moments that shaped the world we know today. It gives you the chance to relive people's journeys, learn from their mistakes, and see the world not only through their eyes but from different vantage points. This book will act as a time machine and take you on a journey to witness Great Britain's history.

This book's journey will first take you back to the intriguing stories of Stonehenge and prehistoric England. You will discover tales of ancient societies and their extraordinary achievements and uncover the mysteries of Stonehenge and how it came to be.

Then, the following chapter will explore the legendary tales of the Vikings. You will learn here about the impact of the Vikings' invasion of the British Isles and the destruction they left behind.

England has gone through various transformations over the years. One of the most influential events in its history was the death of King Edward the Confessor. This set the stage for the Norman Conquests, which included tense and dramatic tales that changed the political landscape of Britain forever.

Another impactful moment in Britain's history was the signing of the Magna Carta and how it changed the political environment in the country. The book presents several stories showing why this document was revolutionary.

The book then takes you to the Hundred Years' War. This was a fascinating and tumultuous period in Britain's history riddled with events, battles, and many remarkable characters about whom people tell stories to this day.

The Tudor era was both captivating and powerful. The stories that took place during this period were filled with love, lust, betrayal, and events that transformed Britain in many ways.

After the Dark Ages, Britain stepped into the Era of Enlightenment, a time of intellectual exploration and cultural evolution. Many of the literary works that you read today wouldn't have been possible without all the events that took place in that era. The book presents you with stories about thinkers, scientists, and authors who revolutionized Britain during this time.

When the British Empire rose to power, it changed the world. The book takes you on a journey to Africa, India, and many other countries to reveal how Britain's ambitions, conflicts, and adventures influenced the growth of this powerful empire.

Britain played a big role in both World Wars. The book tells stories of the experiences and bravery of the British soldiers and the people during these tough times.

The last part of the book focuses on Britain's modern history. You will find stories about significant events in Britain whose influence still echoes in British culture.

History is more than stories about ancient events. Everything that took place in the past is relevant today. So, buckle up and get ready for an adventurous journey back in time that will show you how Britain's past has shaped its present.

Chapter 1: Stories on Stonehenge and Prehistoric England

Stonehenge is an incredible sight to witness. It is one of the most popular monuments in the world, with thousands of tourists visiting it every day. Throughout the centuries, Stonehenge has been linked to mythology and even magic. Many legends and folklore surround this fascinating monument. It was once claimed that Stonehenge was built by none other than the Arthurian wizard Merlin. Others also believe that the stones have healing and magical powers. To this day, Stonehenge still fills people with curiosity and wonder, and they always come up with theories to try and solve its mystery. Some of these theories are interesting, while others may seem far-fetched, almost like a plot for a science fiction movie. For instance, some people believe it is a female fertility symbol. However, others believe it was once a landing area for an alien spacecraft.

Although these are all fun and thought-provoking theories to entertain, Stonehenge isn't magic or a place for extra-terrestrials to park their spacecraft. So why does this monument spark people's imagination? What is its origin and history? This is what you will discover and more in this chapter.

It has been around for thousands of years and took over 1500 years to finish.[1]

1. The Origins and Construction of Stonehenge

Similar to the pyramids of Giza, Stonehenge is filled with secrets and raises more questions than answers. 5,000 years ago, ancient Britons built this monument on Salisbury Plain. Since they didn't have the modern technology that we do today to create a monument of that size, the construction process took about 1500 years and went through multiple phases.

It all started with the Neolithic Britons digging a huge circular ditch on Salisbury Plain. A few centuries later, builders raised 83 bluestones in a circular or horseshoe shape. These stones came to be known as Stonehenge. Sadly, only 43 of them have survived the test of time.

These stones have been standing tall for centuries, piquing people's interest with questions about who built them and why. During the 12th century, the ancient Britons were under the impression that the legend of King Arthur was factual. So, they believed that Merlin created Stonehenge. However, the monument was built centuries before the story of Merlin and King Arthur came to be.

Stonehenge has also been associated with the Celts and their priests, the Druids. However, the stones were built hundreds of years before the arrival of the Celts. So, who built Stonehenge? It was built by a group of tribes, contributing to several phases throughout the centuries to create this work of art.

The purpose of Stonehenge is one of the biggest mysteries in the world. The only way to answer this question is to invent a time machine and ask the ancient Britons themselves. However, many theories hold merit.

Judging from the placement of the stones, it is believed they acted as a solar calendar, and astronomers used them to mark the four seasons. However, recent discoveries suggest that the area was a burial ground for the ancient Britons and a temple to honor their dead and connect with their departed ancestors.

Archeologists also discovered ancient human remains that showed signs of illness and injury. This led them to speculate that ancient Britons believed Stonehenge was a place for treating ailments. When they fell sick, they traveled to Stonehenge, seeking the blue stones' healing powers.

One of the most fascinating and beautiful theories about Stonehenge is that it represents the unity of Great Britain. During the construction, people came from every part of the island to work on creating this masterpiece. This theory makes the most sense for various reasons. The construction of Stonehenge took resources and manpower that required the help of many people on the island. Thousands of people brought the stones from Wales and worked together to place them in the right spot and erect them. Stonehenge serves as a reminder of a time when the British people let go of all their differences to create something that could last until the end of time.

This next theory is pretty entertaining. It is believed that aliens visited Earth, shared their knowledge with the ancient Britons, and helped them create a model of the solar system, which came to be known as Stonehenge.

Stonehenge can have more than one purpose. It has been around for thousands of years and took over 1500 years to finish. It makes sense that people used it for many different reasons.

2. Druid Connection with Stonehenge

The Druids were high priests who lived among the Celts and acted as mediators between the gods and the people. They were educated and well respected by all of Britain. They practiced Druidry, a spiritual belief that revolves around the sacredness of nature. Hence, they performed many of their rituals outdoors in various locations. Was Stonehenge one of these locations?

For centuries, ancient Druids have been associated with Stonehenge. Perhaps the mystery behind Stonehenge and the mystery of the Druids led people to come up with their own theories and believe that these ancient priests built Stonehenge.

It has been established that the Druids didn't build Stonehenge since they weren't around during its construction. There is also no evidence to suggest that they practiced rituals there.

So, how are the Druids connected to Stonehenge? Well, they aren't. The Druids worshiped their gods and practiced rituals in groves. There is no evidence associating the Druids with Stonehenge or any other stone monument.

The misconception could also be related to the modern Druids who feel connected to Stonehenge and often practice their rituals there. However, their practices differ from those of their ancestors since this revival movement took place centuries after the ancient Druids disappeared.

If there is nothing linking the ancient Druids with Stonehenge, why do many people believe they are connected? When it was discovered that prehistoric Britons built Stonehenge, the Druids were ancient pagan priests who lived in Britain, so people assumed that the ancient Druids built it. However, with the advancement of technology, archeologists discovered that Stonehenge predates the Druids.

Some of the modern Druids who brought back Druidry also studied Stonehenge and found it to be the perfect place to practice their new faith. So, the ancient monument is connected to the revived Druidry, not the ancient practices. Since many people don't know the difference between modern and ancient Druids, this led them to believe that all Druids are connected to Stonehenge.

Another reason for this misconception was the book publishers. Authors who wrote about Stonehenge struggled to find publishers for their books. Some writers added the Druids into their books and linked them to Stonehenge to make it more interesting. This tactic worked, and many writers got the chance to publish their work, like William Stukeley, author of "Stonehenge: A Temple Restored to the British Druids." The information in that book and others like it wasn't 100% accurate and contributed to the spread of this misinformation.

Even though Stonehenge isn't associated with any religious movement, it still has a spiritual significance. Pagans from all over the world visit this site every year to connect with nature and practice their beliefs. Thanks to the mystery and mythology surrounding Stonehenge, many people believe that it holds spiritual and magical powers connecting them to their gods and the spirits of their loved ones.

Pagans consider Stonehenge to be a sacred place where they can call on the spirits of their ancestors and become one with nature. Many people believe that these stones have healing powers, and many go there for clarity and guidance. Pagans and non-pagans feel their energy shift after visiting Stonehenge as the place leaves them feeling lighter and motivated.

The shapes and colors of the stones are also meant to honor deities like Thor, the Norse god of thunder. This strengthens the belief that Stonehenge is a temple and a place for worship.

Whatever a person's beliefs are, they usually experience a spiritual awakening at Stonehenge.

3. The Beaker Folk

In 2,500 BC, many people migrated to Great Britain, and they were called "The Beaker Folk." They were given this name because their potter vessels resembled the shape of a beaker. When they first arrived in Britain, their numbers were small; however, the Beaker Folk managed to become landowners in a short time and control many parts of the region. They were archers, farmers, aristocrats, and the first metalsmiths in Britain.

The Beaker Folk had a significant influence on ancient Britain. They were the first people in the country to work with bronze. They introduced alcoholic beverages and woven garments and were famous for making pottery, some of which are still intact and displayed as artifacts in British museums.

Since many of them were farmers, the Beaker Folk paid a lot of attention to agriculture. They cultivated more lands to accommodate the country's growing population and took advantage of marginal lands that many farmers ignored. They also changed the common societal orientation during the Neolithic Era, called for equality, and introduced patriarchies in the Bronze Era, when kings and tribal chiefs were given special treatment.

The Beaker Folk transformed Britain, and it is impossible to imagine what the country would have been like if they hadn't migrated there.

You are probably wondering how the Beaker Folk relates to Stonehenge's history. The Beaker Folk were prehistoric people living in Britain prior to the construction of Stonehenge. It is believed that they were the ones who built the historic monuments. Looking at their history and influence over Britain, it is clear that they had the skills and resources to create such a complex masterpiece.

The Beaker Folk were extremely smart and ahead of their time. They were skilled metalworkers, highly artistic, and exceptional potters, so they were qualified to create something that survived the test of time, like Stonehenge. The Beaker Folk left their mark on Great Britain by leaving behind their metalwork and pottery. However, Stonehenge showed the world their true genius. Even though the Beaker Folk are long gone, their legacy will forever be remembered through Stonehenge.

When the Beaker Folk arrived in Britain during the Stone Age, they considered Stonehenge a sacred place and used it to bury their dead.

Between 2,400 and 2,200 BC, they continued the work of the Neolithic Agrarians, who laid the foundation of the monument in the first phase. The Beaker Folk started the second phase by erecting 82 bluestones in the area. They brought these stones from Wales. Archaeologists discovered that Stonehenge was first built in Wales. The bluestones were considered sacred, and the Welsh highly venerated them. However, the Beaker Folk dismantled the stones and brought them to Salisbury, where they are still standing.

This was a tough journey, and it took the Beaker Folk hundreds of years to finish Stonehenge. It isn't clear why they moved the monument from Wales to Salisbury. Whatever their reasons were, they definitely managed to create a mysterious monument that people still wonder about to this day.

4. Prehistoric Britain Life

Unfortunately, there aren't any written records about the lives of prehistoric Britain and how the people lived their lives. All the information available today comes from archeological findings. They found bits and pieces in various places around Britain and put them together like puzzle pieces, giving them an idea of what the lives of the ancient Britons were like.

The first people in prehistoric Britain were hunters and gatherers. They fed off plants and animals like pigs and cattle but avoided wild animals like wolves and bears. Many of Britain's early visitors led a nomadic lifestyle. However, archaeologists discovered ancient huts that date back to 9,500 BC. This indicates that many of them settled in and made the island their home.

In 4,000 BC, many young farmers migrated to Britain from various parts of Europe. At the time, Britain wasn't familiar with agriculture, so the arrival of these folks changed Britain forever and contributed to increasing its population.

The farmers cultivated land and grew various crops like wheat, barley, and pulses. However, many people had no interest in agriculture and preferred to live a nomadic lifestyle and hunt for animals.

With the rise of agriculture, Britain could offer resources for many individuals looking for a place to settle. More and more people, like the Gauls, Celts, and Belgae, were moving to the island. Britain – which was once empty – was now filled with people from different cultures and ethnicities.

The Celts had the biggest impact on the country. They introduced their own mythology and legends that inspired many of the great literary works you continue to read today. They also created fascinating characters like the banshee and leprechaun, still a part of today's lore and folktales.

In the Bronze Age, ancient Britons were introduced to weaponry, jewelry, and beaker pottery, which came with the arrival of the Beaker Folk. Archaeologists discovered these items in ancient graves as people were buried with many of their belongings so they could use them in the afterlife. This indicates that the prehistoric Britons believed in life after death.

The rich were buried near Stonehenge in fancy graves with luxurious goods. The difference between the graves of the rich and the poor was probably influenced by the Beaker Folk and their patriarchal society.

They used cattle to pull carts during that time because horses weren't domesticated until the Iron Age. They highly relied on dogs for hunting, shepherding, and guarding. They made clothes out of animal leather and learned to sew them using needles made from animal bones. They also lived in rounded houses in villages.

In the Iron Age, the ancient Britons began manufacturing iron tools and weapons. This was a significant time for them that had a huge impact on the country's history. During this time, the Romans invaded Britain, and Julius Caesar provided the world with the first written records of the ancient British. He was the first person to write about the Druids and describe their power and influence over the people. However, one shouldn't take his accounts at face value. The ancient Britons and their kings listened to the Druids and considered them leaders and teachers. This was a problem for the Romans, who wanted to take control of the country. So, Caesar might have provided false accounts to destroy the Druids' reputation.

He also pointed out the difference between the lives of the people of Britain before and after 47 BC. People used to lead a primitive lifestyle and lived on animal flesh and milk, but later became civilized.

Unfortunately, there aren't more written records about prehistoric Britain. Some of the information is based on the accounts of Julius Caesar, which many believe to be exaggerated. Thanks to the discovery of archaeologists, the world has an accurate picture of the lives of the ancient Britons.

5. Stonehenge Astronomical Features

The world will never stop trying to figure out the mystery of Stonehenge. It is fascinating, and archaeologists are constantly discovering more of its secrets. One of the most intriguing aspects of Stonehenge is its astronomical features. It observes moon cycles, eclipses, solstices, and many other astronomical events.

The stones are aligned in such a way that if a person sits at Stonehenge's center, they will see the summer solstice sunrise over its heel stone. During winter, one could see the solstice sunset between the tallest trilithons. However, this would be impossible to witness now since half of the trilithon has fallen.

One of the main purposes behind Stonehenge is to observe the solstices and the sun's movements throughout the day.

It was significant for prehistoric Britons to mark the sun's movements, judging by the effort and time it took to transport the stones and place each one in the right spot. Farmers and herders also needed to keep track of the changing seasons so they could determine the appropriate time to plant their crops.

Ancient Britons focused more on midwinter celebrations than midsummer. Archaeologists found evidence that they held feasts at Stonehenge, and people would gather to eat and celebrate. These festivals often took place during the darkest and coldest days of the year. They were meant to honor the sun to guarantee its return in the spring.

It is understandable why prehistoric Britons wanted to mark the sun's movements, but why were celestial events like the eclipse significant to them? Many ancient cultures, like the Neolithic culture, believed that these occurrences were a sign from their deities that could foretell various events in their lives. For instance, powerful celestial events like the solar and lunar eclipse symbolize chaos. When the sky turned dark in the middle of the day, it meant there was a disruption in the universe's natural order.

Stonehenge is an architectural masterpiece that was ahead of its time. During a period when people didn't have the technology or any of the resources one has today, they managed to design a display of stones and place them in a certain way to mark the movements of the moon and the sun. The monument also acted as a calendar to let them know the beginning of each season and even predict celestial occurrences.

Stonehenge is covered with mystery. It could be a solar calendar, a burial ground, a place to perform rituals and connect with the divine, or maybe the aliens built it. It could be all these things, some of them, or it could be something else entirely.

However, one thing everyone agrees on is that Stonehenge is a spiritual place. Whatever your beliefs, you will always feel something different when you are surrounded by these stones. Could this be its main purpose all along? Did the Beaker Folk build it to give people a unique spiritual experience? Maybe one day, someone will discover a way that could answer all these questions. A time machine, perhaps?

Chapter 2: Stories on the Invasion of the Vikings

At the mention of the word "Vikings," different people give varying reactions based on their knowledge of that culture. The Vikings are heavily depicted in many modern-day documentation, whether poetry, archeology, sagas, or even common proverbs. History buffs usually approach the subject with equal amounts of trepidation and fascination with the enchanting and bloody chronicles of the Norsemen. Motion picture enthusiasts are more lenient when it comes to depicting the ways of the Scandinavian raiders as a direct result of several enticing productions such as Vikings and the 13th Warrior. In all cases, there is no doubt that the Vikings' presence impacted the way we perceive the history of many European nations, most of all modern-day United Kingdom.

Historians identify Vikings as Scandinavian pagans that hail from the North (Denmark, Norway, Sweden). They were famous for their rugged appearance, hostile behavior, and tribal culture. They were skilled sailors who moved swiftly through any body of water and settled in lands yet undiscovered. The Vikings left their mark throughout Europe, yet not always in a positive way. While they were excellent traders, they were equally proficient in raiding, pirating, and pillaging.

The Vikings left their mark throughout Europe.'

At the time when the Norsemen set their eyes on Britain near the end of the 8th century, the island wasn't as unified as it is now. In fact, the land was divided into kingdoms separated by the socio-political and economic disturbances that were caused by the Roman departure at the beginning of the 5th century. These kingdoms also included immigrants from Scandinavia and northern Europe and were called the Anglo-Saxon Kingdoms. They included Wessex in the southwest, Mercia in the Midlands, North Umbria in the north (reaching as far as southern Scotland), and finally, East Anglia, currently referred to as Norfolk and Suffolk.

It is safe to say that none of these kingdoms expected the devastation and momentous change that befell them at the hands of the Vikings.

6. The Raid on Lindisfarne

The Vikings set their eyes on the wealthy, easily accessible coastal lands of the Anglo-Saxons and set sail. Anglo-Saxon writers reminisce about the period preceding the assault, saying, "immense whirlwinds, flashes of lightning, and fiery dragons were seen flying in the air," which was considered a dark omen ushering ill fortune. The shores of Wessex were no stranger to the raids of the Vikings. Earlier in 789 AD, three Northern ships landed and killed the king's reeve (a local administrative agent), who had been sent to bring them to the West Saxon court. However, the attack in 793 AD left a deeper impact.

June of 793 AD marked the beginning of the heathens' invasion and settlement in Britain. It was said that three Viking ships approached the shores of Lindisfarne on the northeast coast of England. The abbey's reeve mistakenly believed that they were traders who'd lost their way and made his way to assist them up the coast to the location he thought they were meant to set at. As he got close, the sailors attacked and killed him. They then went on to pillage the abbey and murder all of the island's inhabitants.

This assault varied from its earlier counterparts, as this was no ordinary land they attacked. Lindisfarne was the most sacred heart of North Umbria, the Holy Island, for this is where Christianity laid its roots in the nation. It was where the body of Cuthbert the Bishop was revered as a saint. The Christian monastery was desecrated, the shrine defiled, and the monks were enslaved and put to the sword. It was such a vicious attack that some Medieval writers believed it was God's punishment for their sins.

News of the bloody attack reached Alcuin, a Northumbrian scholar who lived in the Frankish Kingdom and taught King Charlemagne's children. Appalled by the events that had unfolded, Alcuin wrote to the Bishop of Lindisfarne, Higbald, saying,

"Either this is the beginning of greater tribulation, or else the sins of the inhabitants have called it upon them. Truly, it has not happened by chance, but it is a sign that it was well-merited by someone. But now, you who are left, stand manfully, fight bravely, and defend the camp of God."

He pressed on, asking Higbald to look for the reasons why God would allow such a violation of the sacred ground, implying that it was an act of holy vengeance. As the Viking attacks went on targeting holy entities, he continued to press monks and priests not to give in to the pagans.

Following the attack, several religious artifacts, including the body of Cuthbert, were relocated repeatedly to keep them safe from the Vikings.

The attack on North Umbria was a strategic success as the area had been plagued with a five-year period of harrowing tales of betrayal and royal assassinations, and that's when the Norsemen attacked. Economically, it was known for its wealthy monks, and archeological evidence suggests that it was a thriving community with enormous estates littering the mainland, probably housing the biggest Medieval population in the north of York. So, in the eyes of the Vikings, it was an easy treasure to grab.

7. Tale of Ragnar Lothbrok and His Sons

The fable of Ragnar and his sons is a mystical mix of legend and history. The story itself was recited for 350 years long after he was believed to have died. Ragnar had many titles: the whip of England and France, the father of the Great Heathen Army, and the lover of Queen Aslaug. He was one of the main influences that painted the modern archetypal idea of what the Vikings were like.

Ragnar was a Danish royal, son of King Sigurd of Sweden. Two main accounts delve into his life: the Icelandic Sagas and the Danish Gesta Danorum. The Sagas focus more on his domestic life but fail to mention his first wife, Lagertha, who is mentioned in the Danorum. In the latter, it is said that he went to war with the King of Sweden, Froh, who had killed the Norwegian King, Siward, and enslaved the women in his family to work in a brothel. As Ragnar attacked to avenge the murdered king, the enslaved women, clad in men's clothes, fought by his side, taking down King Froh. It is believed that one of these women was Lagertha, his first wife. Impressed by her swordsmanship and courage, he decided to court her, though when he tried to call on her at her home, he found it guarded with a bear and a hound. Undeterred, he slayed the beasts, making quite an impression on Lagertha, who then agreed to be his wife. They had three children together: a son, Fridleif, and two daughters whose names are not mentioned. In the years to come, it is believed that he divorced Lagertha for setting beasts upon him, a notion that greatly angered him. He took a second wife, Thora Borgarhjort, daughter of the king of Sweden, and had several children with her. It was said that he won her hand by fighting two snakes that guarded her house, wearing protective clothes that earned him the name "Hairy Breeches" or "Lodbrok." His third wife, Aslaug, was probably the most renowned, as she gave him three sons who went on to gain more fame and glory than he ever had. His sons, Bjorn Ironside, Ivar the Boneless, and Sigurd Snake-in-the-Eye (and in other recounted tales, he had two others, Halfdan Ragarsson and Ubbe), were master tacticians and warriors with their own tales and adventures.

Driven by his ego and in an effort to prove that he was as good as, if not far better than, his sons, Ragnar decided to go on a conquering voyage to England, which would soon prove to be a horrible tactic on his behalf. In his conquest, Ragnar only sailed with two ships worth of soldiers. When he arrived, he was demolished by the forces of King Aella, who outnumbered him. It is said that he met his doom when he was thrown into a pit of snakes, but not before saying his famous words, "How the little piglets would grunt if they knew how the old boar suffers," foreseeing the arrival of the Great Heathen Army to the shores of England.

Shortly after, the army arrived, led by his sons, Ivar the Boneless, Sigurd, and Ubba (who may or may not have been Ragnar's son). They triumphed and conquered Northumbria, avenging their father's death in the most epic way possible. King Aella was defeated in the battle of York in 867 AD, paving the way for his sons to move further south into the land, eventually killing King Edmund (Edmund the martyr) of East Anglia by 869 AD.

There is no telling how much of these tales are true, as some of Ragnar's exploits are believed to be fantastical fabrications and urban legends. While this may be the case, there is historical evidence of the legendary deeds and adventures of Ragnar's sons.

8. The Great Heathen Army

The coasts of Britain were accustomed to raids from Norse seafarers. It was not uncommon for Vikings to plunder and pillage British soils every summer for as far back as 787 AD, even before the Lindisfarne attack. However, the invasion in 865 AD was no ordinary hit-and-run raid, nor did the soldiers who arrived intend to accept a Danegeld (a payment the English were taxed in exchange for protection). This invasion had its eyes on the land rather than just filling their coffers.

There are two intertwined tales describing the arrival of the Great Heathen Army. The first, which is more recognized, states that the Norsemen tribes had gathered under one banner, "The Raven Banner," after reaching the conclusion that uniting their army would reap more than the occasional portable wealth. They also believed that banding together would make it easier to conquer the disbanded kingdoms of England. They were not wrong.

The Raven Banner's flag depicted a raven flying upwards and was called Hrafnsmerki. The raven was thought to represent Odin, the Chief Viking god of the Norsemen, as he was often pictured with two ravens, Huginn and Munnin. They also believed that when their time came to leave the earth, ravens guided them to Valhalla (the Viking afterlife).

The number of troops that participated in the invasion has been under a lot of scrutiny. While many historians strongly believe they were in the thousands (probably 3,000), others argue that there is no evidence of this number based on the designs of the raiders' ships and that they were probably around 900 in total.

The fictional tale is more poetic, as it paints a picture of the three sons of Ragnar Lothbrok arriving on the shores of Britain to avenge their father's death at the hands of King Aella. This story is less plausible than the previous one because modern-day historians believe Ragnar raided Paris and settled in Ireland while the Great Army ventured from the east coast, but it does cast a whimsical air on the campaign. In the sagas, it is said that they defeated King Aella, and as punishment for killing their father, they performed the brutal and graphic Blood Eagle method of execution on him. The two stories do agree on one thing, though, which is that the leaders of the army, Ivor the Boneless, Halfdan Ragnarsoon, Bjorn Ironside, and Ubbe were the children of the Norse leader Ragnar Lothbrok.

The army spent the winter in East Anglia, where they reached a peaceful compromise stating that they would spare the locals if they provided them with horses. They headed North to Northumbria as winter broke to face King Osberht and King Aella of Bamborough. Following a swift victory, they secured York and placed a puppet leader under their service. They then headed south in 869 AD to conquer Edward the Martyr, defeating his forces in no time. The king faced a rather unpleasant ending, as he was tied to a tree and peppered with arrows for standing firm and true to his Christian faith.

In high spirits from their most recent victories, the Vikings then directed their attention to Wessex, where they faced King Alfred the Great. The battle of Ashdown was not as easy or pleasant as the previous battles they had fought. In fact, the fighting continued for around two years, all through 871 and 872 AD, during which the two armies faced off several times, and Wessex remained unconquered. King Alfred paid Danegeld to his foes in order to buy himself time before the next invasion. In 874 AD, the great army invaded Mercia, driving King Burgred out and cutting off Wessex's last support.

The army then split into two: one half went northward to raid Scotland led by Halfdan, and the other half moved south under the leadership of Guthrum, continuing the raids on Wessex. The final defeat of the great army at the hands of Alfred the Great came at the battle of Edington in Wiltshire. Following the defeat, Guthrum was baptized. A treaty was struck between the two parties, "The Treaty of Alfred and Guthrum," identifying the boundaries of their territories and agreeing to engage in peaceful trade.

This was the start of the Viking settlement in England and the transition from pirates to land owners. Halfland returned south, and the remaining army divided Northumbria among themselves and started plowing and planting the land, nurturing their own farms, forever intermingling with the English culture and influencing it.

9. Creation of the Danelaw

The Danelaw refers to the piece of land that the Danes settled on following the treaty brokered between Guthrum and Alfred. Guthrum converted to Christianity and was granted the name Aesthelstan, while King Alfred served as his godfather.

The Danelaw consisted of five main boroughs in the area of east Mercia. They were Derby, Leicester, Lincoln, Nottingham, and Stamford, with the center of power being in York (Jorvik). Each borough was independent and ruled by a Jarl, with the higher class in Jorvik holding most of the power. The Danelaw covered a huge area of England that today comprises 15 shire counties: Leicester, York, Nottingham, Derby, Lincoln, Essex, Cambridge, Suffolk, Norfolk, Northampton, Huntingdon, Bedford, Hertford, Middlesex, and Buckingham.

Following the treaty's guidelines, this area was where the laws, traditions, and customs of the Vikings held sway. It also detailed steps to reduce the hostility between the two parties and allow for the exchange of trade.

The Danes were also paid Danegeld, protection money in the form of tax, that prevented them from attacking English territories between the 9th and 11th centuries.

Migrants moved from Scandinavia to live and settle in Danelaw, marrying into families of the Vikings. Norsemen rulers started minting their own coins and integrating social statures, mimicking the culture in Scandinavia. Some historians suggest that the Danelaw secured more freedom and maintained the rights of people.

One of the most important settlements was Nottingham, where Ivar the Boneless and Halfland Ragnarsson settled. For a good 80 years, there was peace between the Vikings and the Anglo-Saxons as they co-existed side by side.

As time passed, it was inevitable that this peace would come to an end. Alfred the Great had used the time to fortify and rebuild his armies and strongholds. His eldest daughter, Aethelfaed, and her brother, King Edward the Elder, led the assault on the Vikings to restore the lands occupied by the raiders. In 911 AD, Aethelfaed took over the governing of Mercia and became the lady of Mercians, establishing a burh nearby and starting to campaign against the Danish. She attacked the borough of Derby in 917 AD, bringing it back into the English fold.

In 954 AD, the five boroughs fell to King Edmund, and the Danelaw era came to a close after the defeat of Eric Bloodaxe, the Viking King of Northumbria, returning the land to English jurisdiction.

10. King Alfred the Great's Epic Struggle against the Vikings

King Alfred of Wessex was one of the only English rulers who succeeded in holding his ground against the Great Heathen Army.

The king was born in Wantage, Berkshire, in the year 849 AD. He was the youngest of five sons to King Aethelwulf, Lord of the West Saxons. Faced with the Viking's imminent invasion, through mutual agreement, the brothers came to the strategic decision with their father to rule in succession to each other instead of handing the kingdom over to one child.

A young prince at the time, it was said that in order to gather the sums to defend the land, he rode to a pierced Sarsen stone, known as the "Blowing Stone," and used it to encourage the people to defend their lands against the raiders. He secured a victory in the battle of Ashdown after a ferociously fought uphill assault. Unfortunately, the triumph was short-lived. By Easter, a defeat by the Vikings and the death of his brother followed.

Following the death of his older brother Aethelred, Alfred inherited both the crown of Wessex and the war with the Pagans. Young as he was (aged 22), he was one of the last remaining resistances in the face of the Norsemen's invasion, and he was not backing down. The young king was forced to pay off the Danes with Danegeld to buy himself time until he could rally his forces once again and force the heathen army to retreat to Mercian London. The Danes continued pillaging Dorset, breaking their oaths to the English and their own Gods (Thor).

In January of 878 AD, Guthrum, the Viking leader, attacked the king while he was celebrating the 12th night in Chippenham and laid waste to everyone he could find. Alfred managed to survive the attack and started planning his revenge upon reaching the conclusion that the Danes could not be bought; they had to be conquered.

He assembled a fort 60 miles southwest of Chippenham on the central Somerset Isle of Athelney. He gathered all the remaining soldiers still loyal to his cause from Somerset, Wiltshire, and Hampshire and marched to meet Guthrum in the Village of Edington. To say the battle that ensued was bloody is an understatement. The white horse of Westbury commemorated the battle, saying, "At last, he gained the victory. He overthrew the Pagans with great slaughter and smiting the fugitives; he pursued them as far as the fortress."

Following the battle, Guthrum held out in his own stronghold for two weeks, finally submitting to King Alfred the Great and agreeing to the Treaty of Wedmore (also known as the Treaty of Alfred and Guthrum), which led to his baptism and the establishment of the Danelaw.

King Alfred's reign lasted from 871 AD to 899 AD.

Chapter 3: Stories on the Norman Conquest of 1066

The Norman Conquest of England in 1066 was one of human history's greatest and bloodiest conquests. It claimed the lives of over 100,000 people, many of whom were civilians. It brought about several changes to the traditional English way of life; some were for the good of the country, while others were not.

The Anglo-Saxons, who ruled England for more than 600 years, were brought down from their elite status. The English language encountered a sudden influx of French words and phrases. The high-powered Anglo-Saxons in the government were replaced with Normans, and the laws were rewritten in Latin from Old English. The Normans also mingled with the native English people, and intermarriages became common practice. Most importantly, slavery was abolished in English society.

It all began when the English king, Edward the Confessor, met with the Duke of Normandy, William I, sometime during his reign.

The Norman Conquest of England in 1066 was one of the greatest and bloodiest conquests in human history.[8]

11. The Succession Crisis and the Battle of Stamford Bridge

Edward the Confessor was the son of the English king, Æthelred II (978 to 1013 and 1014 to 1016), and his Norman-born wife, Emma. She was the great-aunt of William I, in the sense that she was his grandfather's, Richard II, sister. It made William I a distant cousin of King Edward, very far back in the order of succession. Edward and Emma didn't have any children. Whether they couldn't have a child or didn't want one is a matter of debate. This lack of a direct descendant sparked the succession crisis following King Edward's death in 1066.

The next in line for the throne was Harold Godwinson, the Earl of Wessex and the most powerful aristocrat in the country. The Anglo-Saxon council of the king, the Witenagemot, was responsible for raising Godwinson to the throne and crowning him king. However, it didn't take long for two other rulers to dispute King Harold's ascension. One was the Duke of Normandy, William I, and the other was the Norwegian king, Harald III.

William may have had a weak claim in terms of blood relation to the late king, but he stressed that King Edward had named him his heir with

Godwinson as a witness. King Harold simply dismissed the claims and continued ruling the country.

King Harald Hardrada's challenge of King Harold's crown had nothing to do with the similarity in their names. He was not related to the English kings in any way. The blood of the Vikings ran through his veins. His claim arose from an arrangement between the late Norwegian king, Magnus the Good (1035 to 1047), and one of the previous English kings, Harthacnut (1040 to 1042). They had agreed to let the other's heir rule over both Norway and England if either didn't have a child.

The reality was that Harthacnut had made this agreement when he was King of Denmark. Since he wasn't married and didn't have any children out of wedlock, he had named Magnus his heir. However, Magnus extended his claim to the throne of England during Edward the Confessor's time. He declared war on Edward a few years after he was elected as England's king, but he died under mysterious circumstances. King Harald decided to pick up where Magnus left off after Harold Godwinson was elected as the king of England.

King Harold knew that Duke William was the more dangerous of the two, a keen tactician with a larger and better-equipped army. So, he marched south with a huge army and camped to wait for William to begin his invasion. To his surprise, Harald struck first. Sometime in September, he attacked England from the north with a force of over 15,000. His army included the men of Tostig Godwinson, Harold's brother, who was dismissed from his service early in his reign.

King Harold had to rush northward, during which time Harald had crushed the army of Edwin and Morcar, Harold's brothers-in-law. It was called the Battle of Fulford and was over as soon as it had begun. Nevertheless, the Norwegian king suffered considerable losses during the battle. He later conquered York, where his army rested. It was at this time that King Harold reached their camp with his heavily bolstered force from London (over 15,000 strong).

In the early hours of the morning, Harold launched a surprise attack on the weary and depleted Norwegian army. Their advance was slowed down on the narrow Stamford Bridge, where they had to march in a small file. There, a handful of Vikings held their own against the entire army. Despite the numerical advantage of their enemy, they put up a good fight. This choking setback gave time for the rest of Harald's army to form and gather strength. However, the soldiers had to leave their armor behind due to lack of time.

It is said that the battle raged for hours on end despite the odds being clearly in favor of King Harold. Eventually, as the numbers of the Norsemen dwindled further, their defense faltered. The deaths of Harald and Tostig were the last straw, and despite being reinforced by Eystein Orre's army, who also led them to a final counterattack, the Norwegians were defeated.

More than 80% of their army was put to death. Those who surrendered or were captured, which included Olaf Haraldsson (son of Harald) and Paul Thorfinnsson (Earl of Orkney), took a pledge never to invade England again and were allowed to return to their homeland.

However, the victorious King Harold and his men barely had any time to celebrate. Three days after the Battle of Stamford Bridge, William I began his invasion of England from the south. Emboldened by his victory, Harold was confident of taking on the Duke of Normandy's army. It was William's turn to go down now, or so Harold believed.

12. William I, the Duke of Normandy

William I was born sometime in 1028 to the then Duke of Normandy, Robert I, and Herleva, his chamberlain's daughter. The two had William out of wedlock, and they never married. Robert had another child from a different lover, a daughter named Adelaide. He didn't marry that mistress either, or anyone else for that matter. It left William his only heir for the Duchy, and he proclaimed so before his death in 1035.

William's ascension to Duke wasn't smooth. His young age (around eight years of age) made him a target of many nobles hoping to gain power by controlling him. Since he had the support of the King of France, Henry I, and Archbishop Robert (his great-uncle), he was protected from the political machinations of the nobles during the first two years of his Duchy. However, when the archbishop met his death in 1037, the conniving nobles swooped on the young Duke William like vultures to a dead body.

William's guardianship changed hands quite a few times in the coming years. Every previous guardian was supposedly murdered by the one that followed, from Alan of Brittany to Osbern the Steward. Other important men in the realm – instead of trying to control William, were blatantly opposed to his Duchy. However, it wasn't until 1046 that a real rebellion gathered steam.

Guy of Burgundy, supported by many other Viscounts and nobles, was the leader of this rebellion. William was hidden and protected by his remaining family, in particular his maternal uncle, Walter, and his cousins, William FitzOsbern, Roger de Beaumont, and Roger of Montgomery. Despite their efforts, Guy of Burgundy almost managed to capture the duke.

After the failed attempt, William was given refuge in King Henry's halls, and a year later, he went back to his Duchy with the king's forces (including Henry I himself) to subdue the rebels. Needless to say, he emerged victorious. It didn't mark the end of the rebellion, though. Guy, the leader of the rebellion, was exiled in 1050, but other nobles and lords tried to take his place. It was around the same time that William's partnership with King Henry began to deteriorate.

It so happened that Geoffrey Martel, the Count of Anjou, laid claim over Maine in a direct move against William I and King Henry. Both of them wished to control the county. They managed to remove Geoffrey from Maine, but it wasn't a joint effort. William had come into his own, and he didn't need the support of the French king anymore. His influence in Normandy was growing. In an attempt to regain control of the region, King Henry switched sides and merged his power with Geoffrey Martel.

In 1054, the king and Geoffrey, along with several other nobles, launched an attack on William's duchy. They encroached on the region from two different sides. William was prepared for a possible attack, though. Taking half his army, he pushed King Henry and his men beyond his duchy's borders. His trusted supporters, like Roger of Mortimer and Walter Giffard, defended the other side of the invasion.

King Henry and Geoffrey may have lost one battle, but they had no intention of giving in. They launched another attack on William's duchy three years later, but they were thwarted again. It was time now for William to be on the offensive. He conquered the County of Dreux and laid siege to Thimert-Gâtelles. It was during this siege that King Henry and Geoffrey met their deaths. Then, the balance of power inevitably shifted in William's favor.

It has been claimed that Edward the Confessor probably reached out to Duke William when his duchy achieved stability. The then king of England may or may not have promised William his throne. There were no records of such a conversation, nor was there any confirmation from Harald III to have witnessed the promise. Nevertheless, the Duke of Normandy insists that there is truth to his version of the story.

With such a diverse and lengthy experience of war and politics under his belt, William I was ready to begin his conquest of England and claim his rightful (at least, according to him) throne.

13. The Battle of Hastings

As King Harold patiently waited with his army for William on the southern shores of England in August 1066, the latter's troops were ready to depart from Normandy. However, the fierce winds on the South Sea (now called the English Channel) prevented the Normans from setting sail. Those winds probably changed William's fate because if he had crossed the sea at that time, he would have landed in the waiting arms of King Harold and his large army (twice as large as William's).

The Battle of Stamford had depleted Harold's forces considerably. The surviving soldiers were exhausted and weak, and they didn't have much time to recuperate. Still, their numbers were slightly greater than William's, so it was more or less an even match. The Duke of Normandy's ships docked on the shores of Pevensey, a small village in Sussex. News of their raids in the village reached Harold's ears, and he hastened southward.

Meanwhile, William slowly marched east, raiding towns as he went, until he reached Hastings. There, he built a castle out of wood, which acted as his temporary base. Harold hoped to take the Normans by surprise, but William had scouts set up at discrete points around his base, and they let him know about the arrival of the English army well in advance.

William countered with his very own surprise by launching an attack on the English force, which was set up six miles north of his Hastings base. It was early morning on the 14th of October 1066 that the Norman forces commenced their charge on King Harold's defensive formation.

Their first few strikes were largely unsuccessful against the unshakable shield wall of the English. Many of William's soldiers were impaled on the pikes, which apparently prompted a few others to flee. A considerable number of Harold's soldiers went after the fleeing enemy troops, but as soon as they were out of reach of their main force, the Norman cavalry chased them down and killed them.

William used the same strategy successfully a few more times to chip away at Harold's army until their king was left relatively vulnerable. That was when the Normans struck in full force, and during the skirmish, King Harold was slain. It is unclear who hit the killing blow. From an arrow to the eye to William's broadsword in the gut, reports of Harold's death vary from soldier to soldier.

Some said that Harold didn't even die in the battle and lived on in complete isolation. Regardless of the English king's fate, one thing was as clear as day: William had won the Battle of Hastings and had solidified his claim to the throne of England. Alas, his dream of ruling England was not to be, not yet.

14. The Harrying of the North on King William, the Conqueror

Soon after news of the outcome of the Battle of Hastings reached the Witenagemot, they elected another Anglo-Saxon king, Edgar Ætheling. A furious William marched toward London, crushing any English forces that resisted his advance. No army, no matter how big it was, prevailed against the wrath of the Norman Duke, and eventually, Edgar and his supporters yielded.

William I, the Duke of Normandy, was crowned King of England on the 25th of December 1066. He was the first Norman king of England, William the Conqueror, as he came to be known later. In an attempt to quell any more rebellions, he granted lands to the nobles that revolted against him, including Edgar Ætheling. Thinking his kingship had been solidified in the realm, he went back to reside in Normandy in 1067, taking a few English nobles with him to ensure continued support. However, the rebellions continued.

William's half-brother, Odo (they shared the same mother, Herleva), was left in charge of the kingdom in his absence. During his time, Dover Castle in Kent was attacked by Eustace II of Boulogne, but it was well fortified, so they had to retreat. Eadric the Wild engaged the Norman troops in Hereford. Gytha, the late King Harold's mother, began staging revolts against the usurper from the town of Exeter. Odo was more of a warrior than a politician or a tactician, so he probably didn't know how to handle the rebellions that popped up in many parts of the country. Thus, at some point in December 1067, William had to return to England.

He laid siege to the Gytha's band of rebels and forced their surrender. The dawn of 1068 saw Edwin and Morcar's rebellion in partnership with the Welsh rulers. Even the Earl of North Umbria led a small uprising against the new king. However, William swiftly executed his suppression tactics, and one after the other, the revolters were forced to flee the country.

Nevertheless, rebellions, small and big, continued for a few more years. From the raids in Devon by the late King Harold's sons to the revolution of Sweyn II of Denmark. Through it all, Edwin and Morcar kept troubling William with incessant rebellions until Edwin was killed and Morcar was incarcerated for life.

Later, King Malcolm III of Scotland refused to recognize William's authority over the continent, so the latter had to march northward in 1072. During this time, rebellions cropped up in England again, most of which were taken care of after William returned victorious from Scotland in 1075. The Christmas of that year was a merry one for the Normans when William the Conqueror had finally asserted his control over England and its surrounding regions.

15. Chronicling the Radical Transformation of England

A direct impact of the Norman invasion was the complete eradication of the old English aristocracy. A new hierarchy was established as King William stripped off the lands of the English nobles and gave them to the Normans. English Earls were replaced by Norman Earls, and English sheriffs were replaced by Norman sheriffs.

When William ran out of castles to confer with his Norman followers, he constructed new ones in the form of *motte and bailey* castles. Norman-style Romanesque architecture was introduced in the country, with grand, magnificent structures that overshadowed the old English buildings.

The Catholic Church in England underwent a profound transformation as well. By 1096, barely any Englishmen held high-ranking posts at the church, and the place of God was entirely in control of the Normans.

King William adopted the old English governmental systems because they were effective, but he replaced the English employees with Normans. It was the language that changed drastically, though. All official governmental documents were translated from Old English to Latin. The intermittent usage of French words while speaking English became a common practice. Most of the Norman nobility, including the king himself, used the Norman French language while communicating, which came to be known as the Anglo-Norman dialect. It is said that although William understood English, he could speak in broken sentences at best.

Over 8,000 Normans and continentals emigrated to England from their homeland during William's reign. Most of them married amongst themselves, but quite a few intermarriages were found in the records, especially between Norman men and English women. Intermarriage became common in Norman, England, several decades after William's death.

An indirect consequence of William's conquest of England was the abolition of slavery. It so happened that the Norman-controlled church wasn't comfortable with the costs of maintaining enslaved people. However, slavery wasn't abolished overnight, but as the years went by, fewer and fewer slaves were registered until the 12th century, when not a single enslaved person was to be found in England.

This series of radical transformations didn't sit well with the Anglo-Saxons. Many of them left the country and settled down in Ireland and Scotland. A few English immigrants were also found in Scandinavia.

Despite the ruthless and forceful nature of the Norman Conquest of 1066, it brought about several beneficial changes to England, many of which were there to stay.

Chapter 4: Stories on the Magna Carta

The Magna Carta, also known as the "Great Charter," is one of the most significant documents in English and Western political thought history. It has its roots in the turbulent times of 13th-century England and played a pivotal role in the development of constitutional principles and the limitation of royal power. The Magna Carta was issued on June 15, 1215, during the reign of King John of England. King John's rule was marked by disputes with the nobility, heavy taxation, and a perceived abuse of royal power. In response to growing discontent among

King John's rule was marked by his insatiable greed.'

the barons and nobility, they forced King John to meet them at Runnymede, a meadow near the River Thames, where he agreed to seal the Magna Carta.

The Magna Carta consisted of a series of written promises and agreements between the king and his barons. Its primary purpose was to address grievances and establish certain fundamental principles.

16. The Tyrant King

In world history, there are only a few monarchs as reviled as King John of England. Born in 1166, John was the youngest son of King Henry II and Eleanor of Aquitaine. He was thrust into the tumultuous world of medieval politics from a young age, and his upbringing left a mark on his character. John's nickname, "Lackland," was not a reflection of his wealth but rather a testament to his lack of success in acquiring land compared to his older brothers. From an early age, he harbored a deep-seated resentment toward his family and sought to assert his own dominance. This desire for power and his inherent sense of entitlement would set the stage for a reign marred by tyranny and oppression.

One of the defining characteristics of John's rule was his insatiable greed. He imposed exorbitant taxes on his subjects to fund his military campaigns and extravagant lifestyle, often driving them to destitution. This excessive taxation was not merely an unfortunate necessity but a deliberate policy to enrich the crown at the expense of the people. The common folk were burdened with an unfair tax system that squeezed them dry, while the nobility and clergy enjoyed significant exemptions. John's rapacity extended beyond taxation. He exploited his position to confiscate estates, seize inheritances, and exploit legal loopholes to extort money. This pattern of behavior eroded the trust and loyalty of his subjects, especially the powerful barons who had traditionally supported the monarchy.

The king's propensity for cruelty was also notorious. He was known for his quick temper and willingness to resort to violence to achieve his goals. His treatment of political opponents was often brutal, and he didn't hesitate to use torture to extract information or confessions. Even his own family members, including his wife Isabella of Angoulême, were not immune to his wrath. One of the most infamous incidents that fueled discontent was John's handling of his dispute with Pope Innocent III over the appointment of the Archbishop of Canterbury. In a daring move, the pope placed England under interdict, effectively cutting the country off from the sacraments of the Church. John responded with defiance, confiscating church properties and silencing dissenting voices. This conflict with the papacy further isolated him and weakened his moral standing.

As word of John's tyranny spread throughout the land, opposition began to coalesce around a group of disgruntled barons. The barons, led by figures like Robert Fitzwalter and Stephen Langton, the Archbishop of Canterbury, realized that they could no longer tolerate John's oppressive rule. They began to gather in secret, forming an alliance aimed at confronting the king and demanding justice. In the simmering cauldron of discontent, a rebellion was brewing, ultimately leading to the iconic moment in history when King John would be forced to reckon with the consequences of his actions at the meadow of Runnymede.

17. The Road to Runnymede

The journey to Runnymede was fraught with tension, intrigue, and a sense of impending reckoning. The barons who had united against King John knew that they were embarking on a perilous path. However, their determination to curb the king's unchecked power and establish the principles of justice and fairness in their kingdom drove them forward. Runnymede, a picturesque meadow along the banks of the River Thames, would become the stage for this pivotal moment in English history. As the barons and their advisors converged on this serene location, they were acutely aware of the gravity of their mission. They were demanding not just personal redress but a broader transformation of the political landscape.

The barons arrived at Runnymede with a clear agenda. They were armed with a list of grievances that they believed were the epitome of the wider injustices perpetuated by King John's rule. Foremost among these grievances were the heavy taxation and arbitrary confiscation of property that had left many barons financially crippled. The barons also sought to address the issue of scutage, a tax paid in lieu of military service. John had abused this levy, often demanding exorbitant sums even when there was no immediate threat of war. The barons were determined to curtail this practice and ensure that military service and taxation were fair and proportionate.

Another key concern was the abuse from the royal officials, known as sheriffs, who were responsible for collecting taxes and administering justice in local communities. These officials, appointed by the king, often acted with impunity, engaging in corruption, extortion, and other abuses of power. The barons demanded reforms to ensure accountability and fairness in the administration of justice. At Runnymede, the barons were not alone in their efforts. They were joined by religious leaders, including Archbishop Stephen Langton, who played a pivotal role in mediating the negotiations. Langton, a scholar well-versed in the principles of natural law, saw the opportunity to channel the barons' grievances into a broader framework of justice and human rights.

As the negotiations commenced, emotions ran high among the barons and King John. The barons were resolute in their quest for concessions, while John, aware of his position, was equally determined to maintain his authority. The discussions were characterized by debates, impassioned speeches, and moments of deadlock. In the midst of these negotiations, a council comprising both barons and clergy was established to oversee the process. This council played a role in ensuring that the agreements reached at Runnymede would be adhered to and enforced.

As time went on, it became apparent that a middle ground had to be found. The barons did not seek to overthrow the monarchy; they only aimed to curb the king's powers and safeguard their own rights and privileges. After weeks of negotiations, a preliminary document began taking shape – one that would later be renowned as the Magna Carta.

18. The Day of Destiny

The Day of destiny arrived at Runnymede, casting its light upon the beauty of the English countryside. It was in this tranquil setting that a momentous event would unfold. The barons, along with their advisors and witnesses, gathered around a table to mark this occasion. King John reluctantly stood on one side of his role in this unfolding drama. Though compelled to address the barons' concerns, he remained steadfast in safeguarding the authority of the crown.

Amidst weeks of negotiations, the Magna Carta materialized. Crafted clauses aimed at addressing the grievances of the barons and restraining the king's power were now read aloud. As these clauses echoed through the air, a mix of relief and apprehension filled their hearts. The document commenced by affirming the rights and liberties of the Church - a tribute to leaders who had joined forces with the barons for justice. It then delved into issues concerning taxation - the concern on everyone's mind.

Amongst all its provisions, Clause 12 emerged as one of significance within the Magna Carta. This clause established a principle; no scutage or aid (tax) could be imposed without seeking counsel from all corners of society. Henceforth, arbitrary taxes could no longer be levied by kings without securing consent from their trusted barons and advisors.

It served as a limitation on the king's authority and ensured that taxation would be fairer and more transparent. Other sections addressed the misconduct of sheriffs and established that justice would be administered impartially and without prejudice. Clause 39 proclaimed, "No individual of status shall be detained, imprisoned, dispossessed, banished or harmed in any way unless it is through the lawful judgment of their peers or by the established laws." This particular clause laid down the principle process of safeguarding people from arbitrary arrests and punishments.

As each section of the Magna Carta was read aloud, it received approving nods from the barons and their advisors. They recognized that this document had the potential to transform the relationship between the ruler and his subjects, paving the way for a fairer society. Finally, after all sections were read and agreed upon, it was time for King John to affix his seal on the Magna Carta. As he pressed his seal into the wax, there was a moment of silence, as if even Mother Nature herself held her breath. The ink had barely dried on this parchment; its impact would reverberate throughout history.

The signing of the Magna Carta marked the beginning of an important chapter in English history. It brought about a change in the relationship between the king and his subjects. It established principles such as justice, fairness, and individual rights. This document had an impact on law and governance, shaping their course for years to come.

19. The Birth of Rights

The Magna Carta was not merely a list of objections and demands; it was a profound statement of principles that laid the foundation for the rule of law, individual rights, and constitutional government. Its clauses, carefully crafted at Runnymede, were not just about curbing the excesses of a tyrannical king but about establishing enduring principles that would shape the course of history. Among the most significant clauses was Clause 39, which declared that no free man could be imprisoned except by the lawful judgment of his peers or the law of the land. This clause, often referred to as the "law of the land" or "due process" clause, established a fundamental principle of justice: that individuals had the right to a fair trial and protection from arbitrary punishment.

Clause 12, which mandated that no scutage or aid (tax) could be levied without the common counsel of the kingdom, was a groundbreaking provision that placed limits on the king's power to tax his subjects. It introduced the concept that taxation required the consent of those being taxed, setting the stage for more accountable and representative fiscal policies. Another crucial clause was Clause 40, which ensured that justice would be administered promptly and without delay. It stated, "To no one will we sell to no one will we refuse or delay, right or justice." This principle underlined the importance of a timely and accessible legal system, a key component of a just society.

The Magna Carta also tackled the issue of misconduct among officials, especially the sheriffs who held significant power at the local level. Clause 17 introduced guidelines for appointing sheriffs, ensuring that they were individuals who would carry out their duties impartially. This provision aimed to combat corruption and misuse of power within the justice system. Apart from these clauses, the Magna Carta safeguarded the rights and privileges of groups, including merchants. These clauses acknowledged the importance of freedom and recognized trade as a key factor in the kingdom's prosperity.

While primarily addressing concerns raised by barons, the Magna Carta's principles had an impact on society. It laid down a foundation for law, gradually extending rights and liberties to a broader range of people over time. The Magna Carta was not a fixed document but rather an evolving one, open to revisions and reinterpretations in line with needs. Its lasting legacy lies not only in its clauses but also in its overarching principles of justice, fairness, and individual rights that it championed. These principles would go on to shape law development, not only in England, but across numerous nations worldwide.

20. The Global Legacy

The Magna Carta, born out of the complex political climate of 13th-century England, has left an indelible mark on the world. Its impact transcended its time and place, shaping the development of constitutional principles and legal systems in nations far beyond the borders of England. One of the most remarkable aspects of the Magna Carta's legacy is its profound influence on the formation of the United States of America. The Founding Fathers of the United States, deeply influenced by Enlightenment ideals and a commitment to individual rights, looked to the Magna Carta as a foundational document in the development of their own constitution. The principles of limited government, due process, and the protection of individual liberties found in the Magna Carta resonated strongly with the American colonists as they sought to break free from British rule. The concept that no one, not even a king, was above the law was a fundamental tenet of both the Magna Carta and the U.S. Constitution.

One of the most direct echoes of the Magna Carta in American history is the inclusion of the Fifth Amendment, which guarantees due process of law and protection against self-incrimination. This amendment, along with other elements of the Bill of Rights, reflects the deep-seated belief in individual rights and the rule of law that the Magna Carta helped to popularize. Furthermore, the idea of taxation with representation, a core grievance of the American colonists leading to the American Revolution, was rooted in the Magna Carta's demand for consent in taxation. The cry of "No taxation without representation!" echoed the spirit of Runnymede and was a defining principle in the founding of the United States.

The Magna Carta's influence extends far beyond the English-speaking world. In the aftermath of World War II, the international community came together to draft the Universal Declaration of Human Rights (UDHR). This historic document, adopted by the United Nations General Assembly in 1948, laid out a comprehensive framework for the protection of human rights on a global scale. Eleanor Roosevelt, the driving force behind the UDHR, explicitly acknowledged the Magna Carta's influence on the declaration. The UDHR drew upon centuries of thought on individual rights, and the Magna Carta was a key precursor to this evolving concept. The UDHR enshrined principles such as the right to life, liberty, and security of person, as well as the right to a fair and public trial, echoing the Magna Carta's enduring legacy of justice and rights protection.

The Magna Carta's impact is not limited to the United States and the UDHR. Its principles have reverberated throughout the world, influencing the development of constitutional frameworks in numerous countries. For instance, Canada's constitution, including the Canadian Charter of Rights and Freedoms, incorporates principles inspired by the Magna Carta. The Charter guarantees fundamental rights and freedoms to all Canadians and serves as a cornerstone of the country's legal system. The Australian Constitution reflects the Magna Carta's emphasis on the rule of law and individual rights. It has played a crucial role in shaping Australia's legal and political landscape.

The post-apartheid South African constitution, adopted in 1996, draws from the Magna Carta and other sources of human rights principles. It emphasizes equality, justice, and the protection of individual rights. India's legal system incorporates many elements from British common law, which – in itself – is heavily influenced by the Magna Carta. The Indian Constitution guarantees a range of fundamental rights to its citizens, including equality before the law and protection from discrimination.

Apart from its implications, the Magna Carta is also a representation of broader concepts such as the rule of law and justice. It serves as a reminder that everyone, regardless of their status or authority, must adhere to the law. This principle resonates across cultures and beliefs, providing guidance to those who strive for fairness and accountability in governance. In countries where the rule of law's under threat or human rights are violated, the Magna Carta remains an inspiring source and a rallying cry for justice advocates. Its legacy reminds us that the struggle for rights and freedoms transcends time and place – it is a pursuit that spans generations.

The Magna Carta originated in 13th-century England and has proven to be an enduring document of utmost significance. Its principles have influenced the formation of nations and have served as a benchmark for safeguarding rights. From its inception in Runnymede to its lasting impact on systems, the Magna Carta stands as evidence that individuals and communities possess immense power to challenge tyranny and uphold the values they hold so dear.

Its lasting impact continues to inspire individuals dedicated to creating a society. It serves as a reminder that the pursuit of freedom and commitment to principles is a journey that goes beyond borders and endures throughout generations.

Chapter 5: Stories on the 100 Years' War

If there is anything detrimental in world history that human beings have proven time and time again to be proficient at, it would be wars. The history of humanity is built on conquests and the aftermath of conflict, with civilizations rising and falling like dominoes. Disputes over power, resources, and land have always been a strong enough incentive to shed a fellow man's blood. The story of the 100 Years' War is no different.

Despite its name, the Hundred Years' War didn't last for 100 years; it lasted for 116. From 1337 to 1453, the English and the French went head-to-head over the control of the French throne.

The war lasted for 116 years.[5]

21. Origins of the Conflict

The history of France and England has always been stained with blood. There was barely a period in their joint history where these two countries didn't seize an opportunity to cross swords. Some believe that the seeds of war were planted almost 300 years earlier than its recorded start.

In 1066, the Duke of Normandy (at the time a French province), William, attempted to invade England. At the battle of Hastings, the Duke's army triumphed over the Anglo-Saxons, and he was crowned King William I of England. It's safe to say that this was an unusual situation where a monarch was considered simultaneously a sovereign of England and a liegeman of France. Subsequently, he would control fiefs in France as well. This meant that all future kings of England kept their control and the Dukedom of Normandy. By the year 1154, the English crown's control over the French lands was growing, with King Henry II holding titles like the Duke of Normandy, Count of Anjou, and Duke of Aquitaine, along with his kinsmanship.

This new arrangement remained intact until 1205, when King John lost control of the French lands to the French King Phillip II Augustus. The lands lost to the French were Normandy, Anjou, Aquitaine, Gascony, Poitou, and Maine. This defeat earned King John the nickname Lackland, giving him and his lineage a stronger motivation to reclaim the lost areas. Try as they would to take it back, the French firmly resisted.

Several attempts at peace were made in the coming years to avoid an armed conflict. In 1259, a treaty between Henry III and King Louis IX of France was struck, allowing King Henry control over the province of Guyenne in exchange for the surrender of Anjou, Normandy, and Poitou.

While this treaty seemed like a real path to a truce, it didn't sit well with future generations of both kingdoms, causing more power-grab attempts and more treaties with every passing king.

These little skirmishes continued for a long time, well into the beginning of the 14th Century, ushering in the start of the 100 Years' War.

22. Edward, The Black Prince

In February of 1328, King Charles IV of France died, leaving behind no male heirs to rule. During that time, there were no clear guidelines on how to handle a lack of heirs to the throne. There were, however, two main claims to the throne. The first claim came from the King of England, Edward of Windsor (King Edward III). Like his ancestors, he tried to claim the French crown, and in his declaration, he relied on the concept of inheritance of titles. As it happens, his mother was Isabella of France, daughter of King Philip IV and sister to Charles IV.

The second possible heir was Philip VI, Count of Valois, first cousin of Charles IV, and son of Philip III. Essentially, Edward's maternal uncle.

According to French law, a monarch is to rise to power only if they were related through the paternal side of the previous king, which caused a point of dispute between the two parties. However, in the English rule book, this was not a requisite, for it stated that the blood relation can be maternal or paternal, adding emphasis to the concept of the "blood of kings."

This started a feud between the two candidates, ending in a battle won by the French. It also led to the official declaration of Philip VI as King of France and the unanimous blessing of the French community.

Shortly after this conflict, King Edward was blessed by the arrival of his first son, Edward of Woodstock (later known as the Black Prince), from his wife, Philippa of Hainault. He was born in June of 1330 in Woodstock near Oxford. He received his first armor at the young age of seven, an honor that would shape his life immensely.

The king granted his son funds from the Duchy of Cornwall, making him the Duke of Cornwall along with his other title, Earl of Chester. By 1343, the 13-year-old Prince was granted the title of Prince of Wales.

The Battle of Crécy

In 1337, the conflict heightened between France and England over the claim to the French Throne. It seemed that war was inevitable. The King of England knighted his son and other young knights in July of 1346 to prepare for the war.

Prince Edward was said to have earned the title of the Black Prince from his black armor, while the most favorable theory suggests it came from his "scorched earth" method of war (chevauchée). His technique involved the burning of French Villages and towns and terrorizing the locals, which provided plentiful bounty and food for his troops. It was a well-known method of economic warfare to financially weaken your opponent, making it harder for them to gather and assemble an army from the rubble. It was also a very effective method to provoke King Philip to engage in battle.

In August 1346, the two armies faced off in the battle of Crecy. The Prince was only 16 years old when he led the army's right wing with Sir Godfrey Harcourt. The young Prince fought ferociously against unfavorable odds (12,000 to 25,000). He guided the army into a defensive position on a rise by the river Maine, efficiently employing his Welsh and English archers. The battle was settled in favor of the English, with only 300 English casualties as opposed to the 14,000 fallen French men. The great losses that the French suffered were a direct result of them raising the banner to give no quarter. This resulted in the annihilation of the crème de la crème of the French nobility, including King John of Bohemia, the Count of Blois, and the Count of Flanders.

Following the fateful battle, the Prince earned his spurs (the mark of knighthood that is awarded in a full knighting ceremony). Legend states that following the battle, the Prince assumed the emblem and motto of the fallen Bohemian king, the 3 white Ostrich feathers, and the saying, "Courage, I serve" (homout; ich dene).

In July of 1347, the English king and his black Prince marched with 26,000 soldiers, effectively laying siege to Calais for a whole year before capturing it.

The Battle of Poitiers

King John II was newly crowned the King of France in 1350. Continuing the tradition of his predecessor, he went to war with the English. In a strategic move on the Black Prince's part, he moved in 1355 to raid Gascony and capture Bordeaux, a land that served as a main patron to the French Kings' coffers.

Edward adopted the same strategy of torching cities, farming lands, and villages as he moved forth. Once again, this proved very effective in pushing the unwise King John to engage in battle. A French army was assembled in an effort to cut off the link between the southeast English forces and their counterparts in Normandy. This interception surprised the Black Prince's corps. The battle of Poitiers was fought the next day, on 19th September 1356, in the mixed topography of woods, farmland,

and marshes, 4 miles away from Poitiers. Once again faced with adverse odds (35,000 to 7,000 Englishmen), the Black Prince triumphed over the muddled leadership of the French and, through employing the English longbows to his advantage. Prince Edward captured 2,000 French knights, as well as King John II, who was escorted back to England, where he remained in captivity for four years.

It's important to mention that the Prince was well-known for his manners and proper behavior. He treated his captives with respect and courtesy, displaying chivalry in his actions. Additionally, he generously shared gold among his followers and soldiers while also making donations to the churches in England.

In 1362, the Prince was appointed as the Prince of Aquitaine by his father after their failed attempt to seize the throne in Reims. This particular stronghold proved to be impenetrable in 1359. After enduring a winter during their endeavor, an agreement was reached between the King and England through the signing of the Treaty of Bretigny in 1360, which ensured peace between both nations for a span of two years. Following this period of peace, the Black Prince shifted his focus towards Spain in 1367 by aiding King Pedro the Cruel of Castille against his brother Henry of Trastamara, who had challenged him for the throne. Edward emerged victorious over Henry at Nájera in Castille, and as a token of gratitude, he received a gem known as the Black Prince's Ruby from the King. To this day, it remains part of England's crown jewels.

In 1361, at Windsor Castle, the Prince entered into matrimony with his cousin Joan, who held the title Countess of Kent. The couple had two sons, Edward and Richard, who later became known as Richard II of England. The circumstances surrounding the Black Prince's death are uncertain; some believe it was due to injuries sustained during wars, while others suggest it was an illness. Ultimately, the Prince, who had dedicated a portion of his life in service to the monarchy, passed away before having the opportunity to assume the throne.

23. Joan of Arc

Joan of Arc stands as one of history's greatest female warriors and saints. She was born in Domrémy la Pucelle, France, in January 1412 during the period of the 100 Years War. At that time, England appeared to be gaining the upper hand, asserting control over portions of French territory. This shift in power was largely attributed to King Henry V's triumph at the Battle of Agincourt in 1415.

King Henry V enjoyed a series of victories against the French forces. In 1420, he compelled them to acknowledge his descendants as legitimate heirs to the French throne through the terms outlined in the Treaty of Troyes. Additionally, he forged an alliance by marrying Cathérine of Valois, daughter of the King. This union further solidified his ties with Philip the Good, Duke of Burgundy. However, Charles of Valois' supporters succeeded in assassinating Philip's father.

By 1422, when Henry V tragically passed away, the Anglo-Burgundian Union had firmly established its presence across much of Northern France. The baton was then handed down to his son, Henry VI.

The village where Joan of Arc lived was right at the border of the French lands that the English controlled. At the young age of 13, Joan started experiencing visions and hearing voices. She claimed that those manifestations came to her from St. Michael the Archangel, St. Margaret of Antioch, and St. Catherine of Alexandria. The voices she heard instructed her to give aid to the man who was the rightful heir to the French crown, the dauphin Charles of Valois, son of Charles VI.

The young Prince was growing restless as five years had passed since his father's death, and he was no closer to being crowned. It was tradition to crown the new king in Reims, a land that was currently in the middle of the English territories. As long as the Prince remained unconsecrated, his claim to kinsmanship was open for dispute.

The Siege of Orleans

One of the reasons many believe Joan of Arc was having divine visions was her audience with Prince Charles. In 1428, Joan traveled to meet Charles in a temporary court he had set up in Chinon on the Loire River. She wanted to explain her divine mission to earn him back the throne. After being turned away, she returned with the same claim a year later, convincing the captain to allow her an audience with Charles. Upon meeting the Prince, it is said that she divulged information about him that no one else knew. After further examination and questioning, the young maiden was able to win over the dauphin and his followers.

She was then recruited to provide assistance in Orléans, a French city under siege by the English. Joan dressed herself in white armor, cut her hair short like a man, and headed to Orléans. On her way, she ordered the clergy of St. Catherine's Church to dig up a sword under the stone floor near the altar. No one knows how she knew of the location of the weapon or the story behind it, but a sword was found, nonetheless.

Prior to her arrival in Orléans, Joan sent a letter to the English commander, asking him to gather his soldiers and exit Orléans and France. Though the English didn't take the letter seriously, they considered it an alert to an approaching force. Hundreds of the French troops situated in Blois made their way toward Orléans on 27th April 1429. When Joan arrived with La Hire, one of the French commanders, with supplies, she was advised that any action should be postponed until reinforcements arrived.

The young maiden was resting when she suddenly roused from her sleep, stating that her "counsel" had advised her to attack immediately.

She put on her armor and hurriedly left in the direction of an English fort to the east. When she arrived, she found that an engagement was already taking place, and the French were suffering many casualties. The French troops were inspired and renewed their attack on their enemies upon seeing Joan's arrival. This led to a victory and the French securing the English fort. Following several other battles led by Joan, she freed the city of Orléans and eliminated the English at Patay, earning herself the title of the maid of Orléans. In the battle of Les Tourelles, she was wounded by an arrow but continued to stand her ground until the French secured their victory.

Joan was present during the coronation of the dauphin in July of the same year when he was officially named King Charles VII. Following these victories, the maiden made it clear that she wished to restore all of France, making advances to secure Paris that were, unfortunately, futile.

The End of Joan of Arc

In May of 1430, Joan of Arc was captured by John of Luxembourg in Compiègne, where she was unhorsed and could not remount. News of her capture spread through France, and the King, working towards a truce with the Duke of Burgundy, did not attempt to rescue her. By January of 1431, she was surrendered to the Bishop of Beauvais, Pierre Cauchon, in exchange for 10,000 francs. She was put on trial and accused of over 70 crimes (later reduced to about 12), with heresy and dressing as a man at the top of the list. After being forced to sign a confession denying that she ever received divine visions, she later defied her captors' orders and donned men's clothing again. She was then sentenced to death by burning at the stake on May 30th, 1431.

20 years following her death, King Charles VII ordered a new trial be held where her name was finally cleared.

24. Battle of Agincourt

King Henry V was a well-known antagonist/protagonist during the 100 Years' War, depending on how different people viewed him at the time. The King, continuing the legacy of his predecessors, fought against the French to claim the French crown.

Two months prior to the battle of Agincourt, he had led 11,000 soldiers across the English Channel and laid siege to Harfleur in Normandy. The siege lasted for about five weeks. Many of the King's men were either deserters or became afflicted with disease and battle fatalities. Eventually, they surrendered. The King marched northeast to Calais, where he would meet the English fleet and sail back home.

King Henry, however, didn't anticipate the 20,000 French men intercepting his over-exhausted soldiers in Agincourt on their way home. The battle was a bloodbath, with most of the details of what went down disputed by both parties.

The French force was led by Constable Charles D'Albert and Marshal Jean II Le Meingre.

On 25th October 1415, the battle was held on a muddy field flanked by woods, which minimized the chances of large-scale maneuvers. Henry positioned his archers on either side of his remaining men in arms. At 11 a.m., the French started a slow advancement, weighed down by their heavy armor. The English archers armed with longbows with a range of 250 yards rained hell on the enemy. The French cavalry and knights tried to assert their positions and catch the English off guard but failed miserably. Their predicament arose from the tight, muddy space that wasn't accommodating to their large numbers and the protective stakes that the English archers were shielded behind.

King Henry then ordered his archers to raise their axes and swords and attack the French, essentially creating a bloody massacre. 6,000 French men fell on the battlefield that day, while the English lost about 400, marking this victory as one of the greatest and most impressive encounters in Henry's military history.

Five years later, following several other victories, the French recognized King Henry V as heir to their throne. Unfortunately, he didn't live long to enjoy his triumph as he died two years later from camp fever near Paris.

25. The End of the War

The end of the bloodbath between the English and French came in the battle of Castillon on July 17th, 1453. If a comparison is to be made between the state of the lands before and after the war, it will be noted that almost no change occurred, for most of the areas that the English took possession of were, in the end, reclaimed by the French.

King Henry VI was the first and only English King to receive the honor of coronation in France. Following the crowning of Henry VI (who was 10 years old at the time) in 1431 at the church of Notre Dame, the territories that the English acquired across the channel started to slip through their fingers. By 1436, Paris was retrieved by the French, and by 1450, so was Normandy. In 1451, the French attacked Aquitaine and gained control of Bordeaux, which they had lost 300 years previously to the English.

Loyalists to the English crown traveled from Bordeaux to England, seeking aid from the King.

The English retaliated with 3,000 men under the command of the Earl of Shrewsbury, John Talbot, recovering most of western Gascony in October 1452. In July 1453, the French army faced John Talbot's forces in Castillon, where they defeated him and he was killed.

By October of the same year, it was clear that no more English reinforcements were on the way. And so, the surrender of Bordeaux commenced, and the English left the French lands apart from Calais, which was officially reclaimed in 1558 by the French.

There was one final attempt to attack France in 1475, which quickly dissipated after King Louis XI bribed the English army led by Edward IV to go back home.

The Anglo-French war did not end with a peace treaty or a truce. For some time following the last battle, the French were apprehensive and ready for another English attempt to invade their lands.

Without a doubt, it impacted both nations immensely. Even though both nations suffered numerous losses and had similar societal struggles as a result of the war, these similarities did not bring the two nations any closer together but rather widened the rift that was already there.

As a result of the raids, France was greatly ravaged by the war. They were meant to undermine the French ruler by murdering citizens, torching the crops and houses, and pillaging its riches. The economy was gravely damaged, with taxes on the rise to compensate for the lost funds in the war. However, it wasn't long before the country started rebuilding itself from the rubble. The future French monarchy was quick to assert itself after the recovery of its rightful crown. Meanwhile, the English were enjoying the riches they plundered from France over the course of the war, building churches and new houses.

It is safe to say that patriotism and the national identity in both countries rose after the war, with several generations knowing nothing but the conflict between them. England distanced itself from the rest of Europe, developing parliamentary democracy, despite the English Kings still claiming to be Kings of France all the way until George III.

Chapter 6: Stories on Henry VIII and the Reformation

Most readers find refuge from their daily hectic lives by delving into fantastical modern tales of love, power, and betrayal. However, if examined closely, history provides a bottomless well of unbelievable, incredible stories of romance, greed, and redemption with the most unexpected twists imaginable. These historical characters are not works of a writer's imagination in countless pages of books. They lived, breathed, and thrived on the same earth that humanity inhabits today.

It is wise to consider that not all recorded accounts were documented accurately. Personal gain, ego, and vanity usually lend a hand to the ink painting the pictures of those characters. With this in mind, the story of Henry

The story of Henry VIII continues to be an inspiration to the creative minds of our time.'

VIII continues to be an inspiration to the creative minds of our time. From television and movie interpretations to novel and abstract stories, the tale of Henry's love life entanglements, family, politics, and conquests is, as they say, one for the books. Those who are not into perusing books probably recognize this famous name from the TV show "The Tudors" or the big screen masterpiece "The Other Boleyn Girl." These works of art have transported their viewers into the 16th-century royal palaces of England.

However, one of the most controversial monarchs of England was not actually meant to be king at all. The young prince was the second-born son of Henry VII and was promised a life free of responsibilities and full of pleasures until his brother's untimely death.

Henry Tudor (Henry VII) was one of the last surviving descendants of the House of Lancaster, following the vicious power struggle over the throne during the War of the Roses. Henry VII ascended the throne after defeating Richard III, the last remaining son of the House of York and the Lancasters' sworn enemy.

As a newly ordained King, Henry VII wished to end the ongoing dispute between the English families and decided to wed Elizabeth of York, a well-thought strategic move to reunite the nation economically and politically. Together, they had four children: Arthur, Henry, Margaret, and Mary.

So, who exactly is Henry VIII?

26. Who Is Henry?

Henry VIII made his grand appearance in the world at Greenwich Palace on June 28th of the year 1491. For most of the country and royal family, the young prince was considered the spare royal in case any misfortune was to befall his elder brother. Prince Arthur was growing up to be a bright and sporting young man.

While most historians cannot say for sure whether the brothers were cordial towards one another, it is mentioned that throughout his life, Henry kept his late brother's garter robes with him. Soon after the second heir to the throne was christened, he was sent to live away from his older brother with his sister Margaret at Eltham palace, under the care of his mother.

In 1502, at age 15, Henry's older brother died of an illness that to this day remains a mystery. Overnight, Henry's life was turned upside down.

His father, Henry VII, assigned him several male stewards to prepare the young man for his new duties. Due to a difficult pregnancy, Elizabeth, Henry's mother, rarely spent time with him. By February, the queen had given birth prematurely to a baby girl in the tower of London. Sadly, both mother and daughter passed away days later, renewing the shadow of grief over the royal family.

At the young age of 13, Henry moved to the royal household. His father proved to be an overbearing parent, protective of his only and last male heir. The prince was not allowed to wander alone or hunt or joust without someone accompanying him at all times. These overprotective tactics did nothing for Henry's independence and frustrated him no end. He suffered unpleasant comments from other royals and officials, such as the Spanish ambassador, who remarked that the prince was hidden away like a girl.

This annoying phase didn't last long, though. As he grew older, the young prince flourished. He had a knack for writing poetry and creating music –and was well-versed in subjects. He developed an interest in art. Enjoyed participating in noble sports like wrestling, tennis, falconry, jousting, hunting and sword fighting. It didn't take long for him to earn the titles of a " prince" and a "renaissance man" due to his charm and wit.

In 1509, King Henry VII passed away. At the time, Henry VIII was an impressive 17-year-old with a height of six feet and an athletic build. His rise to the throne marked England's first transfer of power in over a century. His mixed heritage symbolized an era of unity following his father's reign. It is said that upon learning about the public's dissatisfaction with his father's rule, Henry promised conditions to win his people over.

Following tradition, the prince spent the night of his coronation at the Tower of London before being crowned at Westminster Abbey. This act represented not only his ascent to power but also his control over the entire nation.

27. Henry's Romantic Escapades

Henry could probably be named the playboy of the 16th century, with six wives, three legitimate children, and many illegitimate ones, one of whom, Henry Fitzroy, first Duke of Richmond and Somerset, was acknowledged.

Catherine of Aragon

Six weeks following his ascension to the throne, Henry married his late brother's widow. Originally, Catherine, a Spanish Princess, was betrothed to his brother at the age of two, and they wed in 1501 when they were teenagers. A few months later, Arthur met his sudden demise, leaving his widow stranded in England. When Henry became heir to the throne, Catherine was betrothed to him in 1503. They got married in 1509 with a five-year age difference (Catherine was 23, and Henry was 17).

It was uncommon at the time for a brother to take his sibling's widow for a wife. In order to do that, a special pardon had to be granted to the couple from the pope. They remained married for 15 long years, with Catherine giving birth to six children, three sons and three daughters, with only one of the children, Mary 1, surviving in 1526.

By the year 1525, Catherine withdrew more and more from the festive and loud court life that her husband indulged in. She became increasingly pious and reserved. Frustrated with his wife's inability to deliver a male heir and believing that his marriage may be cursed, the king opted to get his marriage annulled so he could take a new wife. This action struck a nerve with the Roman Church, which denied him the right to do so, leading to the church reform in England.

In his demand, the King advocated for separation by using the scripture that indicated that a man cannot wed his brother's wife. Meanwhile, Catherine fought the claim by announcing that she was still a virgin when Arthur died. She was also backed by her nephew, the Holy Roman Emperor Charles, who basically controlled the pope.

After the break from the Roman Catholic Church and their divorce in 1533, Catherine, now called the Princess Dowager of Wales, was ordered out of the royal court. She was forbidden from seeing their daughter Mary and spent the last three years of her life in seclusion with only a few servants waiting on her. She passed away in January of 1536 at Kimbolton Castle and was buried in Peterborough Abbey.

Anne Boleyn

Nearing the end of his marriage to Catherine, Henry became infatuated with one of his wife's ladies-in-waiting, Anne Boleyn.

Anne was one of Sir Thomas Boleyn's daughters. In her youth, she had spent her time in the French court with her sister Mary, one of the mistresses of King Henry VIII. In 1519, Anne was ordered back to

England, with rumors of her promiscuous behavior running wild. She was appointed as one of Queen Catherine's ladies-in-waiting. It wasn't long before the King started to notice her and took her as one of his mistresses. This new development elevated Anne's status. By 1522, she returned to England, becoming a popular figure in court. By 1526, it was a sure fact that the King had become deeply in love with the charismatic young woman.

Henry's close friend, Cardinal Thomas Wolsey, was not a fan of his mistress and called her "the night crow."

In the late 1520s, the King sent numerous letters to Anne, promising her loyalty and love and that she would forevermore be his only mistress.

After the King's seven-year trials to break off dealings with the Roman Church, he managed to wed Anne in 1533. The King divorced Catherine, declaring their marriage null and void due to her relations with his brother, consequently proclaiming his first child, Mary I, illegitimate. All hopes for a male heir now resided with Anne.

In 1533, a pregnant Anne gave birth to her first child, the future Queen Elizabeth I, at Greenwich. Her two later pregnancies, one of which was a boy, ended in miscarriage.

Their marriage lasted for three years, with Ann unable to grant the King a male heir. This failure marked the beginning of Anne's downfall. Supporters of the Old Catholic regime, which the King denounced, exchanged rumors about her fidelity, going as far as accusing her of adultery and forging plans to assassinate the King. The adultery charges were outrageous enough to include relations with her own brother and four other commoners. These rumors were believed to have been brought upon her by Thomas Cromwell and backed by her uncle, the Duke of Norfolk.

In order to acquire a male heir, King Henry VIII accused Anne of treason and practicing witchcraft, sentencing her to death after a sham trial on the 19th of May 1536.

Anne was allowed a small mercy from Henry by performing her execution using a sharp sword instead of an unreliable dull ax.

Jane Seymour

It wasn't long before the King found his third wife. Only 10 days following Anne Boleyn's execution, the King married one of her ladies-in-waiting, Jane Seymour. The wedding took place in Whitehall Palace.

The King finally got his heir and the son that he desired. Jane gave birth to Henry's first male heir, Edward VI, on the 12th of October 1537 at Hampton Court Palace.

Three days following the birth, the young prince was christened in the Chapel Royal. However, tragedy struck the family yet again when Jane suffered postnatal complications and died on October 24th.

The birth of a male heir strengthened Henry's resolve in his choices, believing that he was favored by God now.

Jane was buried at Windsor Castle, becoming the only wife of Henry, who lay in the same tomb with him.

Anne of Cleves

The King remained unmarried for two years after the death of his third wife. As time passed, the ministers felt that the kingdom could possibly do with an alliance with a foreign country. The King decided to send his trusted painter Hans Holbein to the German court to bring him back paintings of the daughters of the Duke of Cleves, Anne, and Amelia. Upon seeing her picture, the King was attracted to Anne, and arrangements were made to seal the union. This marriage can easily be classified as a political tactic to strengthen the ties with Anne's brother, who ruled a protestant duchy in Germany.

Upon meeting Anne, the king was not impressed and started referring to her as "Flanders Mare." He informed his ambassadors and courtiers that he had no interest in performing his marital duties on the grounds of Anne's unfavorable looks. The marriage was soon annulled, and Anne was granted income and several homes in the English country, including Hever Castle. She was a frequent visitor to the Royal court as an honored guest.

Cromwell was not so lucky, though, for the King executed him based on bogus charges of treason for arranging the match.

Kathyrn Howard

Following an accident in one of the tournaments where his horse rolled over him, the King was left with an injured leg. This accident led to him being unable to exercise and thus gaining so much weight he was unable to walk.

At the time, the King was not in a good mental state and longed for a second male heir to secure the succession of the throne. A young, petite, and beautiful Katheryn Howard caught his eye. She was the daughter of the younger brother of the Duke of Norfolk of the powerful Howard family. Katheryn was Anne Boleyn's cousin, and like her cousin, she had a reputation for adultery prior to her marriage to the King.

They sealed their marriage in July 1540, when the King was 49 years old. King Henry was smitten with his new wife, showering her with gifts and calling her "his rose without a thorn." This honeymoon phase didn't last long, though. After two years, the young bride, like his second wife, was accused of infidelity by resuming her relations with an old lover, Thomas Culpepper. The King was heartbroken, and as a result, like her cousin in 1542, she was beheaded at Tower Green.

Catherine Parr

The last love interest and wife of Henry VIII was Catherine Parr. Catherine was just starting a relationship with Thomas Seymour, Jane Seymour's brother, when the King took an interest in her. Catherine was widowed twice by that time and was 31 years old. She was well-educated and clever. She spoke French and Italian fluently and could read Latin. Catherine married the King on July 12th, 1543. She was a devoted wife and a good stepmother to his three children, Mary, Elizabeth, and Edward. Her religious interests in Protestantism almost led to her downfall. These beliefs created many animosities within the royal court. Following a religious debate with the king, he issued a warrant for her arrest on the grounds of heresy. The Queen then hastened to remove all banned religious books and pleaded with the King that her debate was only to distract him from the pain of his injured leg.

As proof of his trust in her, he declared her regent in his absence while on a quest to invade France in 1544, a role that was only held by his first wife, Catherine of Aragon.

28. The Creation of the Church of England

The separation and creation of the Church of England was more of a romantic act than a religious one, with the King wishing to marry Anne Boleyn and divorcing his first wife, Catherine of Aragon. The King was hell-bent on getting his wishes that this predicament was named "the Great Matter." According to the Roman Catholic Church, without Catherine's consent, they were reluctant to annul the marriage. With protestant reformers backing his desires, Henry moved to break away from the Roman Church through a series of acts that were passed between 1532 and 1534.

Following the King's marriage to Anne Boleyn after his new chief advisor Thomas Cromwell (who was appointed after Thomas Wolsey was stripped of all his royal offices for failing to resolve the matter) declared his first marriage annulled, the Roman Pope excommunicated the King in 1533. This was the start of the break with the Roman Church.

In 1533, the English parliament declared the act in restraint of Appeals, which dictated that the Roman Pope no longer had jurisdiction or religious authority in England and that England was an empire. By 1534, the Act of Supremacy was passed, making the King and all his heirs "the Supreme head of the Church of England," which granted him unchallenged power to reform religious institutions. Henry Appointed Thomas Cromwell as vicegerent in spiritual affairs.

Henry was quite pleased with himself at this point; he mixed the faith that he knew as a boy with the salvation he was seeking as a man but without the blessings of a priest. He went as far as demanding that all acknowledge him in place of the pope as God's representative on Earth. Those who opposed him, like Thomas More, were executed for treason at the Tower of London in 1535.

29. The Dissolution of the Monasteries

Following the break with the Roman Church came the dissolution of the monasteries.

Henry started seizing the lands and wealth of the Catholic churches and monasteries in England and selling them off. This motion was led by Thomas Cromwell, who, between 1536 and 1540, demolished, shut, and seized over 800 monasteries and religious houses like Riveaulx, Byland, and Fountains. They went on to accuse the clergy of "Vicious, carnal, and abominable sin."

The riches and money that he acquired from the monasteries were employed in more than one direction. He stored some in the royal treasury, gave some to his new ministers, and used the rest to develop and enlarge the English navy from 5 to 53 ships and build new dockyards. The Mary Rose, one of the ships, lies to this day in the Portsmouth Naval Museum). He made sure to invest in the arts and sciences and the central and local government.

30. Political Conquests

Henry didn't quite fit the archetype of a military commander. However, that didn't stop him from attempting to cement his name as a war hero. Against the advice of his much older and wiser councilors, Henry embarked upon a military adventure with his father-in-law, Ferdinand II of Aragon. In an effort to settle rivalries between the French and the Spanish that were centered on Italian claims, their target was France. The conquest ended shortly in 1520 with a peace treaty with Francis I, King of France. Henry was generous with funding displays and tournaments at the field of the Cloth of Gold, an act to show the unity between the two nations. It is safe to say that his wars with France were rather costly and unnecessary.

Henry did secure a victory in 1513, which was won by the Earl of Surrey, Thomas Howard, against an attempted invasion from the Scots at Flodden.

31. Henry's Death

Henry died at the age of 55 on January 28th, 1547. He was buried next to his third wife, Jane Seymour, in St. George's Chapel at Windsor Castle. He was survived by his last wife, Catherine Parr, who was then free to marry her old lover, Thomas Seymour.

His male heir, Edward VI, ascended the throne at only nine years old but died six years later. He was followed by Mary I, who spent the total of her five reigning years trying to restore the Catholic regime in England. She was then succeeded by Elizabeth I, who restored her father's Protestant vision. Elizabeth was considered the longest monarch to hold the throne of the Tudor Dynasty.

Chapter 7: Stories on the Era of Enlightenment

The English Enlightenment was a time of intense intellectual exploration and cultural evolution. To set the scene, this chapter begins by linking the roots of the Enlightenment to the preceding Scientific Revolution and changes in the cultural milieu. And in order to illuminate this dynamic period of intellectual and cultural evolution, the next story scouts the minds and theories of key Enlightenment thinkers like John Locke and Adam Smith, unraveling their impact on society and subsequent thought.

The third story traces the intensive evolution of modern political theories, explaining how Enlightenment ideas laid their foundations. The penultimate tale explores the vibrant literary culture of the time, focusing on the emergence of satire and notable works of the period. To conclude your journey through the Enlightenment, the last narrative examines the lasting influence of this era on English society, education, and religious perspectives, including the rise of secularism, fully bringing the transformative spirit of the Enlightenment era to life.

Adam Smith – a key figure during the Enlightenment Era.[7]

32. The Roots of the Enlightenment: Scientific Revolution

Preceding the Enlightenment, the Scientific Revolution brought fundamental transformations in theories and philosophies revolving around nature and the universe. Based on the progression principle, which dictates that continuous efforts in scientific research help people understand the words around them, the movement revolutionized scientific methodology between the early 16th and 18th centuries. It also laid the foundations for modern scientific theories and research.

One from whom many British scientists took inspiration was Nicolas Copernicus, the Polish astronomer who first proposed the idea of the Earth revolving around the Sun and not the other way around as previously believed. While shocking to cosmologists at the time, the discovery that the Earth isn't the center of the universe represented a concept that was way beyond the grasp of this scientific field at the time. As a result, people started to question many other long-held traditions and beliefs.

Another groundbreaking theory of the 16th century was the blood circulation thesis proposed by the anatomist Andreas Vesalius. Marking the beginning of the scientific revolution across multiple fields, scientists were now challenging and altering previous conceptions of the universe and society. This was fueled by technical revolutions, which allowed people of all classes to access knowledge and learn about anything that sparked their interest.

After its invention in the 15th century, printing became widespread, disseminating information to the masses. Posters and pamphlets that would inspire countless debates (encouraging people to think more rationally and radically) were printed on a daily basis.

During the Scientific Revolution, one of the figures who had a great impact was Francis Bacon. He is considered the pioneer of the empiricism theory, and he made substantial contributions to learning and knowledge. Bacon introduced a method of research that emphasized continuous observation and logical reasoning to draw conclusions based on what was observed. This approach also allowed for experimentation to either prove or challenge theories. As people became curious about the accuracy of accepted knowledge, traditional beliefs about the universe started being questioned.

Bacon also advocated for the dissemination of knowledge, emphasizing that the government had a role in expanding people's understanding. His colleague, Thomas Hobbes, further supported progress as a means to overcome challenges in comprehending nature.

In parallel, William Gilbert formulated a hypothesis based on magnetism principles, explaining how the Earth rotates on its axis due to forces.

Another influential figure during this period was John Flamsteed, an astronomer from Derby. Flamsteed established "The King's Astronomical Observatory," which became known as the Royal

Greenwich Observatory. Through his expertise and research conducted there, Flamsteed made great contributions in his field. However, his groundbreaking achievement, known as "Historia Coelestis Britannica," was published posthumously.

The contributions of court physician William Harvey were truly groundbreaking and would shape the future of medicine. Through dissections, he comprehensively explained the mechanism of blood circulation. In 1628, he published his findings, elucidating the role of the heart in propelling blood through the system.

During the period of the Civil War (1642-1649), England's Scientific Revolution continued unabated. In fact, after the war's end, there was enthusiasm for embracing science and technology's positive impact on political, social, and economic progress.

In the 1600's, a distinguished body called the Royal Society was established with a mission to advance research across scientific disciplines. It boasted members such as Robert Boyle, Sir William Petty, Sir Christopher Wren, and undoubtedly Sir Isaac Newton – whose monumental works, like "Mathematical Principles of Natural Philosophy" and "Principia" solidified his status as one of the revolution's foremost figures. By 1703, Newton had ascended to become President of the Royal Society.

These publications not only presented a structure for mechanics and formulated laws regarding gravitation and motion, but they also revolutionized people's comprehension of science. The remaining part of the century was characterized by the breakthroughs achieved in the preceding years. Alongside establishing the groundwork for industrialization, these discoveries had an influence on politics and culture, igniting a movement that would shape the nation's destiny for generations to follow. This imminent era, known as the Enlightenment, was about to commence.

33. Minds of Enlightenment Thinkers - John Locke and Adam Smith

There were many English Enlightenment thinkers. Two particularly notable individuals who played a significant role in changing society's perception of long-standing ideas were John Locke and Adam Smith. John Locke is famously associated with the concept of the contract, which aimed to establish an agreement between the government and its citizens outlining their respective responsibilities. Under this agreement, citizens would surrender some privileges for freedom while the government would ensure their safety and protect their rights. Locke arrived at this idea after studying the state of nature, which provided insights into how society operated under laws.

Although others before him had also explored returning society to an established authority-led government era, Locke was unique in successfully pursuing this notion during his time. Unlike his contemporaries who relied on metaphors or their own subjective experiences (as our brains often tend to do), Locke was among the first to transcend these limitations and envision a state.

Therefore, he reached the conclusion that each individual (although this applied to men then) is inherently endowed with a sense of morality rooted in natural rights. However, these morals can become tainted through life experiences. The solution to prevent people from deviating from this order is to establish governing bodies that safeguard their rights and enable them to remain faithful to their principles.

Locke's idea that the government had the duty to uphold the natural rights people are born with was quickly adopted by other European thinkers, including Rousseau, who, putting his own spin on it, proposed that the social context should be based on the general will (a government ruled by a collective, not an individual).

Scotsman Adam Smith is the father of the modern economy. After devoting a considerable amount of time to vigorously studying how markets function, this social scientist came up with several suggestions on how to boost the market, including the concept of free market capitalism. In his most comprehensive work, "The Wealth of Nations," Smith prefaced that if a market could operate without the government's constant interference, this would lead to economic growth of never-before-seen proportions. One of the ways Smith proposed to achieve this prosperous state was by abolishing protectionist taxes and monopolist practices, as these hindered international trade at a higher rate. Smith claimed that without these practices, the market would blossom, bringing greater general prosperity to the entire nation.

Smith transferred the same Enlightenment principles and beliefs to economics as other intellectuals did to politics, science, morals, etc. According to Smith, economics are ruled by the same natural laws that people could easily unveil and explain through rational thinking.

Smith based his confidence in the market's development on his belief that if permitted (not limited by taxes and land monopoly), every citizen would want to put their capital into supporting domestic trade, so there would be no need for import. Seeking only their security and prosperity, individuals would also promote the public interest, much to the benefit of the entire nation. Many view these ideas outlined in Smith's The Wealth of Nations as a sequel to his previous work, "The Theory of Moral Sentiments," which laid down the foundation of Smith's naturalistic outlook on society's future.

34. Development of Modern Political Theories

From the 1500s, Europe was in a constant state of political upheaval. Religious leaders and monarchs caused numerous conflicts as they fought over resources and territories and tried to impose different versions of Christianity. Britain saw some of the deadliest battles, not to mention their devastating effects, during the early 17th century. One of the consequences of this was the harsh criticism directed toward the religious and political leaders for allowing the continuous conflict and the loss of so many lives. The other one was the birth of sovereignty. European countries could now seize control over what was happening within their borders without another country interfering with their actions. This law of domestic affairs laid the foundations for modern political theories regarding international relations.

John Locke's proclamation that no ruler should have absolute power over their subjects was another prominent change in the English political scene. Instead of referencing commands from God, the leaders were slowly forced to accept that the authority must come from the people. They had no choice. Incited by Locke's and other Enlightenment thinkers' ideas, the masses were prepared to replace the rules with one that would listen to people. It was the birth of democracy as it is known today. It was the first time that leaders were made accountable by their subjects.

Following these revolutionary changes, another shift happened, not just in Britain but all across Europe. Intellectuals started pushing the idea of the separation of power. They argued that by dividing the responsibilities between legislative, judicial, and executive authorities, a much greater balance could be achieved. Besides dismissing the notion of countries led by one leader, Enlightenment thinkers argued against religious interference in state affairs. This idea was bolstered by generations of conflict and the religious influences on political decisions seen on the continent.

John Locke presented the notion that all people possess natural rights to property, liberty, and life from birth. Moreover, people's rights can't be constrained or dismissed by law or any other power. It marked the beginning of a long and still ongoing fight for individual rights. While the campaign led to improved religious tolerance and minorities across Britain gained more liberty to worship, the country still has a long way to go on this front.

In contrast to the era before the Enlightenment in Britain, where inequality was widespread and religious and political leaders enjoyed rights to land ownership, certain professions, and tax exemptions, a new wave of thinkers emerged. They argued that every individual is born equal, so why should some have it all while others struggle to survive? Initially, this notion of "people" only applied to men. Women, enslaved individuals, and ethnic minorities did not enjoy the rights. However, leveraging the effects of the Enlightenment movement, these marginalized groups gradually began advocating for their equality. Remarkable activists like Mary Wollstonecraft and Mary Astell were at the forefront in England, fighting for women's rights alongside men.

Another significant transformation brought about by the Enlightenment was witnessed in politics through free market capitalism. Prior to Adam Smith's introduction of this concept, mercantilism prevailed – a system where countries relied on production while limiting imports from abroad. However, Smith's theories on free market capitalism emphasized supply and demand dynamics, stringent regulations, and comparative advantage. This led England and numerous other nations to seize the opportunity for increased wealth through trade. Additionally, it prompted them to forge relationships with one another.

Although the system had its flaws, it served as the basis for future trade policies.

35. The Vibrant Literary Culture of the Enlightenment

The British Enlightenment's achievements weren't only limited to the political scene and scientific fields. They also made their way into English literary culture. The 18th-century writers achieved accomplishments in many domains, including periodicals, novels, drama writing, and poetry.

Many authors even started crossing the divide between fact and fiction in their writing. Sir Walter Scott was one of the pioneers in historical novel writing, combining his knowledge of history with plenty of imaginative license.

While unimaginable before, even travel writers started to take the liberty to engage their descriptions with creative fictitious techniques. James Bruce was particularly successful in this genre. However, this was also due to his previously established good reputation, as the introduction of fiction made many readers question the author's authority.

Tobias Smollett, a novelist and a doctor, combined his love for writing with his long-nourished interest in medical practices and foreign cultures. In his works, he explores the use of herbal medicine in different cultures. Likewise, John Gabriel Stedman's accounts of his experiences in the Dutch colony of Surinam paint a fascinating picture of the local, national, and global literary networks established in the 18th century.

Besides the vibrant book culture contributed to by published authors from several genres, the English Enlightenment period is also known for its abundantly consumed literature. This allowed the readers to make the connection between elite and popular culture, which people created since the movement's beginning. As in neighboring Scotland, where ballads played a crucial role in crossing the divide between the different sides of the cultural hierarchy, literary achievements in Britain made people more hopeful of ending inequality.

Another literary field that rose to popularity in the 18th century was satire. The ecclesiastical genre was particularly widespread, often sparking debates among the supporters of the different branches of Christianity trying to establish authority at the time.

Drama and rhetoric also played critical roles in the era. Several plays were created around philosophical concepts introduced during the Enlightenment. The authors often followed the most popular Enlightenment theories so they could provide a faithful rendition of human nature and revolutionary communication methods. Others explored the questions of human nature through science, particularly psychology.

The second half of the Enlightenment's literary culture is loaded with equally illuminating and intriguing works, often focusing on the mysteries of space. However, the author wasn't the only one benefiting from the proof, inspiring enlightened ideas, and the interest these sparked in the public. Publishers also capitalized on other writers' successes, often making a fortune on one or more better-selling publications. This continued well into the next century. Emulating earlier works, publishers often re-made older editions and established collections of authors' works to continue capitalizing on revolutionary ideas of the Enlightenment.

The influence of the vast amount of literary achievements in the Enlightenment continued to inspire authors even in the Romantic era. Moreover, numerous writers across France cited some English authors of the movement. The French were particularly engrossed by 18th-century English poems that captivated their audience with very subtle techniques.

British Enlightenment literary influences are also seen in American literature. The first American novel, William Hill Brown's "The Power of Sympathy" (1789), is full of Enlightenment ideas. The Enlightened literary culture also influenced some of Britain's most renowned early 19th-century novels. Austen, Scott, and Dickens were famous for creating plots around *a mutual duty*, one of the key motivational concepts that pushed the Enlightenment movement forward.

36. The Lasting Influence of the Enlightenment on English Society

The new and exciting ideas of the Enlightenment spread like wildfire across Britain. At first, the royals and the church tried to censor and even ban public demonstrations of enlightened thinking, along with books and other publications. They were alarmed because they saw people questioning everything wrong with the government and considering changes. Their fears eventually materialized when the concept of the social contract was proposed, inferring that authoritarian leaders could no longer rule without their decisions being questioned by their subjects. After the French and American revolutions, the religious leaders and monarchs lost their supreme authority. While they were still respected by English society, their influence wasn't even a fraction of what it once was.

The theories of ethics and psychology proposed by enlightened thinkers also had a lasting influence. With the popularization of natural sciences, philosophers started to take vastly different approaches to their thinking. Applying rules of natural phenomena to societal issues became a commonality. John Locke's argument that people are subject to the laws of nature just like every other creature influenced England's political scene for years to come. While this prominent impact was also aided by the efforts of Rousseau and other Enlightenment thinkers outside Britain and their influence on Europe's and the United States' political changes, Locke inspired many of them in the first place.

On the purely science front, the Enlightenment led to the theories of deduction and induction and, ultimately, the creation of a very different cosmology than was known before. Based on this, mathematicians proposed that everything in this world operates by a few universal rights. Since then, many of these laws have been discovered, proven, and used to create the biggest masterpieces of mankind.

Enlightenment also encourages people to seek rational reasons behind everything, including religion. This is how deism, atheism, materialism, skepticism, and other radical concepts related to religious belief came to be.

The extreme notions put an end to the Enlightenment. As the new cultural force named Romanticism emerged, people started to turn away from radical and rationalist ideas. It allowed people to explore emotional concepts rather than relying solely on reason. Still, the high optimism brought on by the radical changes of the Enlightenment remained. The British People now knew that progress was possible if there was enough force to prompt it, and this is one of the Enlightenment's most enduring legacies.

Chapter 8: Stories on the Rise of the Empire

This chapter delves into the ambitious imperial interests of Great Britain. You will learn about three of the most significant events of world history, how they contributed to the rise of the British Empire, and how they affected other parts of the world. This chapter explores the conflicts, causes, and aftermaths of the Scramble for Africa, the East India Company, and the Opium Wars.

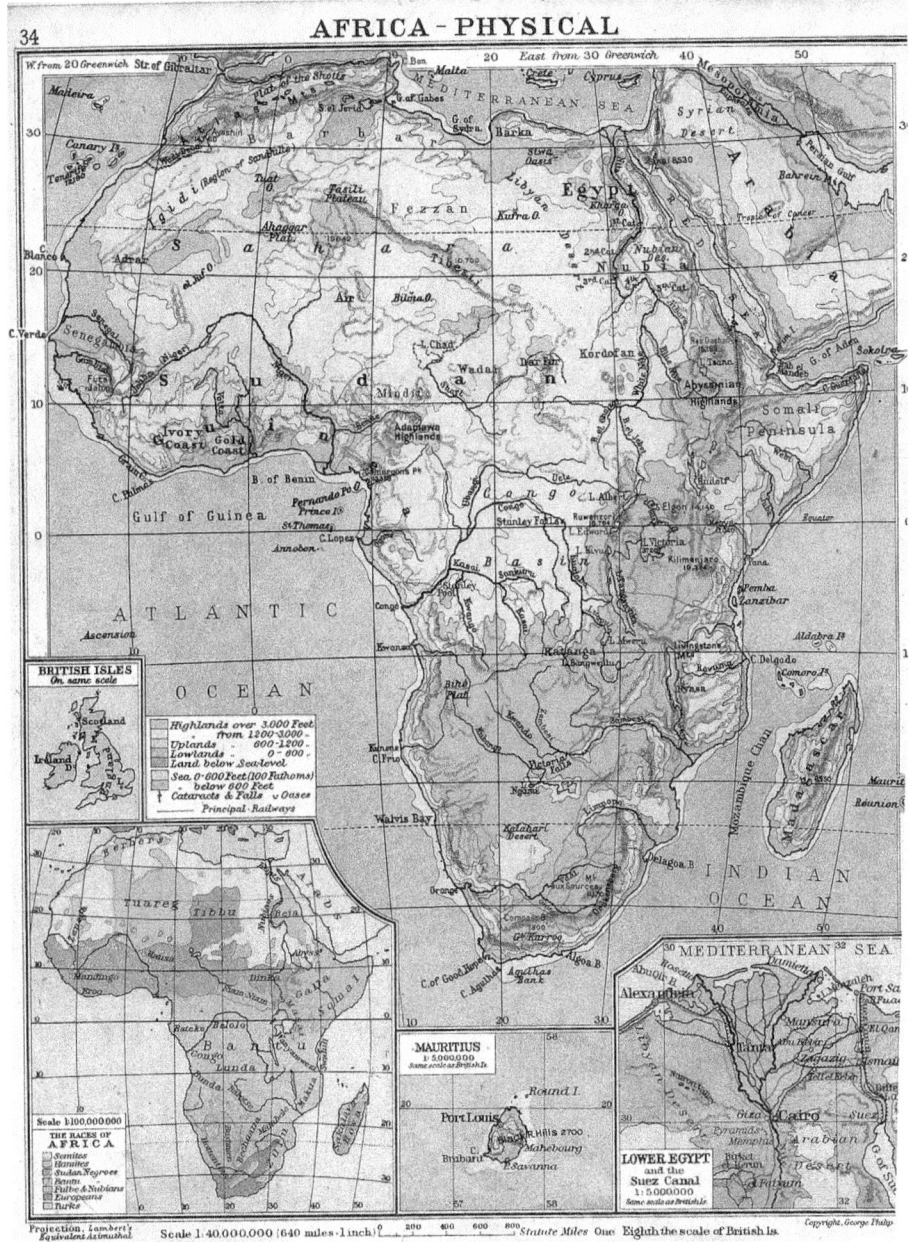

AFRICA - PHYSICAL

Africa was a rich cultural center.'

37. The Scramble for Africa

Starting in the late 19th century and ending in the early 20th century, the Scramble for Africa was a period that shaped the world's geopolitics for years to come. At this time, European colonizers moved at a rapid rate and grew their empires extensively. Contrary to popular belief, Africa, before it was subject to European encroachment, was a rich cultural center.

Colonizers' excuse for invading Africa was that they wanted to "civilize" the continent. While Europe was more technologically advanced at the time, Africa was deprived of the opportunity to utilize its resources to thrive and develop. If it hadn't been robbed of its natural and human resources, the continent would eventually have incorporated European technological and industrial advancements and even built on them.

Before the Europeans arrived in Africa, the continent was home to numerous empires, cultures, and societies, each with its own efficient economic and political systems. In the West lay the wealthy Mali and powerful Songhai empires. In the East, there was the beautiful Swahili Coast. In Central Sudan, there was the prosperous Hausa Kingdom, which was known for being a flourishing trade center, and in the North of Africa, Carthage and the Ancient Egyptian civilization were already making history.

While it wasn't until the Scramble that Europe overtook Africa, Europeans were already sneaking their way through the continent centuries back. For instance, the trans-Atlantic slave trade started when Europeans began their exploration expeditions in the 15th century. There were also interactions between both continents through the trans-Saharan trade routes. These transactions contributed to Europe's expanding influence.

The Causes of the Scramble for Africa

The Industrial Revolution was among the key factors resulting in the Scramble. As demand and supply increased during the Industrial Revolution and rapid economic growth, Europe needed access to more raw materials to keep up. Africa was targeted because it was rich in diamonds, rubber, gold, cocoa, cotton, and other sought-after materials.

At some point during the industrialization, the supply exceeded the population's demand, which is why Europe needed to find new markets to sell their goods. Africa was the ideal marketplace because of its large population. The Europeans would also be introducing new goods to Africa, which people would be curious about and excited to buy.

At the time, the prestige and prowess of a nation were determined by the size of its empire. Dominating Africa benefited Europe's perceived status and geopolitical strategies. Europeans established their military bases in Africa after the colonization. This domination also allowed them to secure profitable trade routes.

Europe's advanced weaponry and strong military power made it easy for them to gain control over Africa, where they still relied on primitive weaponry. They also made innovations in transportation and were skilled at navigation, which aided land exploration. Europeans were able to survive the rough African living conditions with their medical advances.

The Berlin Conference: How Colonial Powers Divided Africa

Africa was officially divided among the interested colonial powers in the Berlin Conference, which took place in 1884 and 1885. The conference was led by Otto von Bismarck, who was a German Chancellor and was attended by European and American representatives. This conference was held to dissipate the rising tension, which might have slowly escalated into armed conflict between nations who wanted territorial claims over Africa. In this meeting, guidelines and agreements were laid out to solidify each nation's territorial rights. The Congo River basin, which was rich in rubber and ivory, making it highly coveted, was declared a free-trade zone to which all colonial powers had access.

This conference led to the exploitation of Africa's land and resulted in the death of millions of its people. Africa was regarded as no more than a commodity that Europeans could divide, share, and rob. No one cared about the continent's inhabitants, traditions, religions, or cultures. Colonizers never involved African representatives in these discussions.

Countries that treated their colonies as extensions of their nations, such as France, spread their cultures, beliefs, laws, and languages there. Others, such as Britain, used indirect means of ruling. Instead of implementing their laws and government structure, they retained the existing power dynamic. British officials were ranked higher than indigenous leaders, who then served as intermediaries between the British government and the people. They made sure that everyone followed the government's rules. The United Kingdom and Great Britain were among the most powerful colonial powers in the Scramble. Its colonies extended all over the region and included Kenya, South Africa, Uganda, Ghana, Nigeria, Sudan, and several others.

The Exploitation of the People and the Land

The economic system that the colonials implemented in Africa was designed to ensure that the continent's resources benefited European commerce and trade. They extracted a wide range of precious metals and stones, numerous agricultural products, and even forced human labor. The African population suffered from food shortages because they were obligated to grow crops that generated profit rather than food crops. Many colonials implemented cruel forced labor systems. King Leopold II of Belgium was known for being the most brutal, as his tactics resulted in the death of millions of workers.

Africans eventually adopted their colonizers' languages, which included French, English, Dutch, and Portuguese. Christianity also spread throughout the continent as missionaries actively converted them, encouraging them to let go of their traditional religions. Some colonials created educational systems for the African population. However, these were not intended to teach them important skills and information but to mold them into an obedient workforce. This limited the skills and education of the population, which is a problem that lasted even after decolonization.

Resilience and Rebellion

Africans frequently resisted and rebelled against the colonizers despite the brutal punishment and treatment they would receive. At first, they resisted by engaging in armed conflict. The Battle of Adwa, which occurred in Ethiopia in 1896, the several wars led by the Xhosa and Zulu people, and the Maji Maji Rebellion that took place in Tanzania between 1905 and 1907 are among the most notable uprisings.

As powerful African leaders emerged, the resistance movements started becoming more powerful and organized. African societies realized that armed conflict wasn't their strongest suit, which is why they started utilizing political strategies instead. During the early 20th century, the African population began advocating for civil and constitutional rights. A few decades later, they also started the fight for independence.

The Decolonization of Africa

World War II and its aftermath and consequences were the main factors influencing the decolonization of Africa. European powers were significantly weakened after the war in terms of military power, political strength, and the economy. This hindered their ability to effectively maintain their policy. The underlying notion of the Scramble that deemed the Europeans racially superior to Africans was also discredited during the war.

There was also a redistribution of global power following the war, with the Soviet Union and the US emerging as the most powerful. The US supported the decolonization of Africa because it was similar to the nation's past fight against colonialism, while the Soviet Union supported decolonization as an opportunity to spread socialist beliefs and stand against Western influence.

Many colonies fought for their independence through atrocious wars, such as Mozambique and Angola, which were Portuguese colonies, and Algeria, which was ruled by French powers; others were decolonized peacefully. While other African countries, such as Egypt, broke away from British control earlier, Ghana was the first sub-Saharan country to break free in 1957, allowing other British colonies to follow with ease.

The French, however, implemented an "association" policy, which encouraged integration and cultural exchange. This allowed their colonies to gain political independence while still maintaining aspects of the French culture and language and keeping economic ties with the nation. The UK was also keen on maintaining strong cultural, economic, and political relations with its formal colonies. They usually continued to invest in these nations and offer assistance with development. The British Commonwealth was primarily responsible for maintaining these ties.

38. The East India Company

The East India Company was also popularly known as the English East India Company. It was established on December 31, 1600, mainly to exploit and monopolize all trade with India, East Asia, and Southeast Asia. This monopolistic entity helped expand the British Imperial interest in Asia. Britain also established the company to get a share of the East Indian spice trade, which was very profitable and was monopolized by Spain and Portugal until 1588.

The company encountered a lot of resistance from the Portuguese and the Dutch, who occupied Indonesia then but were eventually allowed to trade. Its commerce activities started with South Indian goods like silk, saltpeter, cotton, and spices but soon branched out to benefit from trades in Southeast Asia, East Asia, and the Persian Gulf.

The East India Company made use of slave labor from the 1620s to the 1770s. They transported enslaved Africans to India, Southeast Asia, and St. Helena Island to increase production and profits. Enslaved individuals were mostly from East African countries, particularly Madagascar and Mozambique. During the late 18th century, however, the interest in cotton goods declined, and the British developed a liking for Chinese tea. They financed these imports with illegal opium trades, which resulted in the outburst of the Opium Wars in 1839.

The East India Company then faced a lot of backlash for monopolizing the market, giving rise to a rival company. This competition didn't last long, as both entities merged and created the United Company of Merchants of England in 1708. The company had a court that consisted of 24 directors and was organized into several committees. As shareholders could vote on important regulations and changes, they could influence trade policies. However, many problems arose, leading to government intervention. The government established acts that gave them control of political policy. They created a regulatory board that responded to parliament, which resulted in the gradual loss of the company's control over commerce and trade. The company was no longer monopolistic and only a managing tool for India's British government. The company was dissolved in 1873.

39. The Opium Wars

The mid-19th century witnessed a turning point in history known as the Opium Wars. China engaged in the Opium War with Great Britain from 1839 to 1842 and confronted both Great Britain and France in a second conflict from 1856 to 1860. Unfortunately, China experienced defeat in both wars leading to severe consequences. As a result, they were compelled to cede Hong Kong to the powers and establish treaty ports for trade, thereby granting special privileges to foreigners. Additionally, it is worth noting that the British authorities actively facilitated and encouraged the trade of opium among citizens under the guise of free trade.

The First Opium War

Numerous Asian countries, such as India, Vietnam, Malaysia, Vietnam, and Burma, experienced the consequences of the expanding dominance of powers. Despite the influence exerted by the United States, France, Great Britain, and other colonial powers on China's affairs, China itself was never formally colonized. While Confucianism permeated all spheres of governance, society, and culture, unlike resistance movements, it faced less opposition from colonial powers due to its secular nature.

While Great Britain believed that Confucianism wouldn't stand in the way of modernity as some religions did, China wasn't entirely effective in responding to the colonial efforts of Westernization. China was already a bureaucratic, mercantilist country characterized by its military strength and advances in industrialism. Everything about China's social, cultural, economic, and political dynamics was drastically different from the systems of European powers at the time, making it really difficult for the people to deal constructively with encroachment. This caused internal upheaval and political conflicts, repetitive external invasions, and unfair treaties.

During the years that preceded the first opium war, China-based its trade operations with the West in the city of Guangzhou. This was the only place in China in which licensed merchants could trade with foreigners. Great Britain adhered to this trade system for years, as it offered Indian Cotton and British Silver to China in exchange for tea, porcelain, silk, and other goods. While the British enjoyed Chinese goods, the Chinese weren't very interested in British goods, which caused Britain to replace cotton with opium, also from India. The balance was now shifted in Britain's favor, and the Chinese became the ones who had to pay for goods using silver.

Opium was being used for both medical and recreational purposes in China and other parts of Eurasia. To capitalize on this interest in the product, Britain invested more money in opium plantations and processing. They eventually monopolized the industry of opium cultivation and trade. As their investments increased, more Chinese citizens started smoking opium for recreational purposes, which became a widespread addiction. In 1800, the Chinese government recognized that it was a serious issue and banned the production and importation of the product. By 1813, the smoking of opium was outlawed, and whoever was caught smoking it was subject to harsh punishment.

The British still found ways to transport opium to China through private British and American traders who sold it to Chinese smugglers. The Chinese opium trade picked up in 1830, but the British East India Company lost its monopoly over the drug four years later. This caused the price of British opium to decrease, making it more attainable and widespread among Chinese citizens. Members of the government and army, and even those who were studying to take up political and military positions, smoked opium, too. In 1836, the Chinese government went as far as executing Chinese smugglers and dealers.

Over time, the opium issue grew out of hand. Officials were torn between taking the pragmatic approach, which was legalizing the use of opium and applying tax laws on the product, and taking a harsher approach, which involved punishing imported and sold opium. The latter approach was eventually implemented and led by Lin Zexu, a Chinese government official.

Lin tackled the opium issue through many phases. He started by writing an open letter to Queen Victoria in which he questioned British morals. He then arrested over 1,600 Chinese opium dealers and destroyed thousands of drug pipes. He also asked foreign companies to hand over the opium inventories in exchange for Chinese tea. When they refused, Lin ceased all foreign trade and quarantined the area where the foreign merchants were. After a month and a half in confinement, the foreign merchants finally gave up over 20,000 chests of the drug. Lin's troops also seized the opium that was found on British ships around Chinese islands. He mixed the drug with lime and salt to damage its effectiveness before dumping it into the sea. With pressure from Lin, the British ended up moving to Hong Kong after they were expelled from Macao, a Portuguese colony,

All of these events caused British dignity to take a hit, giving rise to the first Opium War. The British government vowed to compensate merchants for their opium losses, which were worth millions of sterling pounds. This gave Great Britain the excuse to expand their colonies into China. The war officially started when conflict arose between British merchants and Chinese warships in 1839. A year later, a British fleet arrived at Guangzhou and started battling, bombarding and invading cities, and negotiating their way through China. China was forced to give up Hong Kong to Great Britain in a settlement. The nation also had to pay reparations and establish full diplomatic relations with the British Empire. As a consequence, the Chinese government also had to send Lin Zexu into exile. The Chinese forces had weaker and less advanced naval ships and weaponry, making them unable to fight against the British forces.

The war ended in 1842 with the Treaty of Nanjing, which was in favor of the British. This treaty gave Great Britain access to five Chinese ports and a profitable port in Hong Kong, which were also now subject to British laws. China was also forced to pay compensation and apply any rights that foreign countries gained to Britain. China, however, didn't receive any benefits from this treaty.

The Second Opium War

The second Opium War started in 1856 when Beijing was encroached on by French and British invaders. New treaties and compensations that harmed China, along with the legalization of the opium trade, were also in effect. In 1856, the Chinese authorities arrested Chinese people who worked on a British ship and executed a French missionary around the same time. Britain and France used these incidents as opportunities to get China involved in more trade. In 1858, China agreed to fulfill several Western demands. However, they refused to sign the treaty, which worsened their situation.

British and French armies invaded Beijing and tore down the Imperial Summer Palace in 1860. The Emperor then fled to Manchuria while his brother negotiated with the French and British authorities in the Convention of Beijing. He signed the treaty, agreed to compensation, and gave up the Kowloon Peninsula to the British.

The Scramble for Africa, the East India Company, and the Opium Wars are among the most significant events in world history that resulted in far-reaching consequences. Great Britain's ambitious imperial interests and its desire to grow its power across continents were what fueled these events. Great Britain's influence played a great role in shaping today's global geopolitics.

Chapter 9: Stories on the World Wars

The two World Wars had a huge impact on history and led to the collapse of many empires. It is impossible to talk about these wars without mentioning Britain's role in them. This chapter covers some of the most interesting stories that took place in the World Wars.

Britain had a vital role to play during WWI and WWII.'

40. The Christmas Truce of 1914

Nobody understands the struggles of war like the brave soldiers fighting and the innocent civilians caught in its wake. In the midst of World War I, British soldiers held onto hope to spend Christmas with their loved ones. However, the intensity of battle forced them to fight for their survival during the holiday season.

On Christmas Eve, British and French troops found themselves huddled together, reminiscing about their families and friends left behind. Then something remarkable unfolded – a moment that could only be described as a Christmas miracle.

Before midnight struck, an unfamiliar sound reached their ears. Usually accustomed to explosions, gunfire, and anguished cries during wartime, this sound was different – it carried a soothing melody.

As they strained to listen, they discovered it was the German soldiers singing "Stille Nacht," their rendition of "Silent Night." Like their counterparts, these German soldiers were also yearning for home and missing their loved ones dearly; thus, they resorted to carols in an attempt to evoke the spirit of Christmas.

Without hesitation or reservation, British and French troops joined in harmony by singing "Silent Night" in their languages.

They all felt a longing for home and tried to make the best of their terrible situation. It was a moment when these men transcended their roles as soldiers and embraced their shared humanity, coming together to celebrate this sacred night.

Something extraordinary occurred on that night. Amidst the singing of the Allied Forces, another sound broke through. It wasn't a song; it was someone shouting. The singing ceased momentarily as they tried to discern the source of that voice. To their surprise, it came from the enemy line. The words weren't in German. An English shout emerged from one of the soldiers, inviting the troops to "come over here." Cautious, the British soldiers proposed meeting in the middle instead. The intentions of their counterparts were met with skepticism; few could have anticipated what would transpire next – most would have dismissed such a tale as unbelievable.

Both sides ventured into no-man's land with trepidation – uncertainty filled the air as they didn't know what awaited them. As they finally converged, British soldiers found Germans waiting for them. Although they had faced each other in battle several times, this encounter felt entirely different. They gathered not as adversaries - but as men who chose words over bullets to communicate.

With mutual trust growing between them with each moment, both Allied and German soldiers laid down their weapons and warmly shook hands.

They exchanged good wishes for Christmas and then gathered together to sing traditional Christmas songs. They enjoyed the company of one another, sharing laughter and conversation while indulging in cigars, wine, and chocolate -and even exchanging gifts. There was a sense of camaraderie as they played football and proudly displayed family pictures. Some soldiers even shared their addresses, hoping for visits once the war came to an end. In an act of compassion, they also supported each other in burying their fallen comrades.

The soldiers found themselves in a state of disbelief. Hours before, they had been locked in combat. During that brief period, they had become friends who shared stories and laughter. For that one night, all feelings of hatred, anger, and bloodshed were set aside. Instead, there was a connection between human beings who sought solace in each other's presence on this sacred occasion. Amidst the chaos and danger that surrounded them daily on the battlefield, this holy night offered them respite from the deafening explosions and the constant fear for their lives.

However, not everyone among the ranks approved of this truce. Certain sergeants and commanders believed that humanizing their enemies would only lead to complications. By forming connections with these men through shared stories about their families, it would become harder to shoot at faceless foes during conflicts. There was one soldier who accused his comrades of dishonoring themselves by accepting this truce; this man was Adolf Hitler.

No matter who opposed the ceasefire it was crucial for the soldiers to remember their humanity before anything.

41. The Evacuation of Dunkirk

During the events of the Second World War in 1939, Germany made its move by invading Poland. The next year, they expanded their invasion to Belgium. In response to these actions, Britain dispatched the British Expeditionary Force (BEF) to aid France and its allies in the fight against

Germany. These significant events reshaped history and ultimately led to the evacuation of Dunkirk.

On May 10th, 1940, Germany caught the Allied Forces off guard with a surprise attack along the border of Holland. They employed ground assaults, parachute drops, and air raids from all directions. This strategic move was unexpected, not just for the Allies; it also surprised the Germans themselves. Adolf Hitler had reservations about this decision due to its risks but eventually approved it.

The attack left Holland and Belgium in a state of shock, forcing them to surrender. British soldiers stationed in France valiantly fought against attacks until they found themselves gradually retreating towards Dunkirk, a port city in France.

The scene that unfolded in Dunkirk on May 26th, 1940, was distressing beyond words. The cacophony of weaponry reverberated throughout every corner of the city.

The British, French, and Belgian troops found themselves surrounded from all sides. The Allied forces felt trapped with no escape. The beaches of Dunkirk offered no shelter, and the German air forces relentlessly attacked them without mercy.

Britain was determined not to abandon their soldiers and allies. In response, Sir Winston Churchill, the Prime Minister of England at the time, initiated an operation named Dynamo with the objective of rescuing their troops and bringing them home. Every available sea vessel was deployed to Dunkirk, ranging from battle ships to fishing boats. It was a massive undertaking, and both soldiers and civilians alike acted swiftly and selflessly to save their army.

Churchill knew what was at stake here. If this rescue mission failed, Britain and the rest of Europe would fall. So, he desperately needed to rescue his men to save his country.

On May 27th, the first destroyer vessels took the journey to rescue the stranded soldiers. However, German air forces attacked any ship and made it impossible to reach the British troops. Luckily, the British air forces quickly intervened, but the battle was ruthless, and their planes were destroyed. The pilots fell on the beaches of Dunkirk, stranded with the soldiers.

Although it seemed like an impossible situation with the Germans attacking by air and on the ground, the British didn't give up. For nine days, they fought relentlessly under harsh conditions, but their persistence paid off, and Operation Dynamo was a success. They managed to evacuate the British and French soldiers. The mission is often called the "Miracle of Dunkirk" because they were expected to rescue 45,000 soldiers or less. However, they managed to save over 300,000 of the stranded troops from England and France. Sadly, 17,000 soldiers didn't make it.

The Dunkirk Evacuation changed the course of the Second World War. By achieving the impossible, Dunkirk gave the British soldiers and the Allies hope and inspired them to keep fighting. The British people were proud of their troops and supported them during these critical times. The soldiers were now more confident than ever. They had proved Hitler and the Nazis wrong since they believed the British soldiers wouldn't return, but they did. The Allied Forces conquered the Axis Powers (Germany, Italy, and Japan) on D-Day and won World War II.

42. The Battle of the Somme

The Battle of the Somme occurred during World War I and stands out as one of the most devastating conflicts in history. By 1916, British and French forces had engaged in combat for over two years. Both sides possessed immense tactical capabilities, making victory elusive for either party.

In an attempt to weaken their adversaries, the Allied Forces devised a strategy to simultaneously assault the Germans from the north and south, intending to inflict damage to their defenses. British troops held great expectations about this offensive believing it could potentially pave their way to triumph. Little did they suspect that two British soldiers had betrayed them by divulging the plan to their enemies. Consequently, German forces were well aware of the assault, leading them to fortify their defenses and await the Allies' arrival.

Meanwhile, the Germans had formulated their own plan aimed at diverting attention from the impending Allied attack and disrupting their forces. They initiated an offensive against troops stationed near Verdun – a city in France – before any opportunity arose for executing the Allies' intended strategy.

The situation faced by the British was dire. They lacked soldiers for their plan as the French were engaged in the battle at Verdun. Simultaneously, they had to initiate their plan to alleviate pressure on the troops who were defending themselves against German attacks. This played into the hands of the Germans.

Despite the circumstances, British commander Douglas Haig maintained a positive outlook and believed the Allied forces could inflict damage on enemy lines. The plan itself was flawless; it just fell short due to an act of treachery.

On July 1st, 1916, a massive army comprising British soldiers from parts of the Commonwealth (including Canada, New Zealand, Australia, India, and South Africa) was assembled by the Allied Forces. They split into two groups; one launched an attack in the south and managed to harm their adversaries, while the second group attacked in the north but faced less success. Within one hour, 20,000 British soldiers were lost in battle, with another 37,000 suffering injuries. This was only the beginning. The conflict dragged on for five months, resulting in a loss of 600,000 soldiers.

The brave soldiers of the Allied army fought valiantly, seeking to exploit any weaknesses in the enemy's defense. However, the Germans consistently stayed a step ahead, accurately anticipating the British army's every move. On July 19th they launched another assault against the Germans, enduring three days of fighting and suffering another devastating loss. Tragically, 5,000 Australian soldiers lost their lives on this day, marking it as one of the worst moments in Australia's history.

Following the Australians' efforts, the South Africans were eager for their opportunity to prove themselves on the battlefield. The Allied Forces launched an attack against the Germans with hopes of securing their flank. Months of battles ensued, and they ultimately achieved their mission; however, this victory was bittersweet. The South Africans alone mourned the loss of 2,500 soldiers while more Allies also perished.

The British army faced setbacks throughout their campaign. Communication issues plagued them, making it challenging to coordinate attacks. Consequently, there were increased casualties, which forced commanders to halt their offensive and devise an alternative strategy. Unfortunately, during this pause in action, enemy forces capitalized on the opportunity to launch counterattacks, resulting in a prolonged battle that surpassed expectations.

In September, though, fortune smiled upon the Allies as they successfully captured both Guillemont village and Ginchy town from German control. The British forces triumphed in their attack against

German defenses, but these victories were relatively insignificant. They did not significantly impact the enemy's defense. With the soldiers exhausted and disheartened from witnessing the loss of comrades, General Haig had to make the difficult choice to bring an end to the Battle of Somme.

In this battle, neither side emerged victorious, with the Germans suffering a loss of approximately 500,000 soldiers. Despite casualties on both sides, the German defensive line remained unbroken.

43. Britain's Role in the Treaty of Versailles

On 28 June 1919, the Allied forces and Germany signed a peace treaty ending the First World War. This took place at the Palace of Versailles in France. US President Woodrow Wilson, French Prime Minister George Clemenceau, and British Prime Minister David Lloyd George all attended to represent their countries and sign the treaty. The war had caused devastation on both sides, with towns and villages in France and Belgium disappearing completely. British lands, on the other hand, only suffered minimal devastation but many casualties.

The signing of the treaty didn't go smoothly. Emotions were running high, and many people were blaming Germany for the war. French Prime Minister George Clemenceau wanted Germany to pay reparations to the Allied forces for all the damage they had caused. British Prime Minister David Lloyd George had a different opinion. He knew that his people were angry and wanted vengeance for all the casualties Germany had caused. He had promised the British people that he would do whatever it took to make Germany pay. However, that was what he said in public; privately, he didn't want to destroy Germany.

George was worried about the Russian Revolution and its impact on Britain and the rest of Europe. He believed Germany could be their strongest line of defense against communism. If Germany fell, the left could prevail. He agreed that Europe shouldn't go easy on Germany, but destroying it wasn't the best idea.

George was also looking for Britain's best interests. He understood that reconciliation was necessary since Germany was a great trading partner, so its economy must not suffer. He also wanted Germany to remain strong to create a power balance between it and France. If Germany fell, France could be the dominant European power. George also wanted to neutralize the German navy so the British Royal Navy would be the most powerful in Europe.

American President Woodrow Wilson wanted to punish Germany, but not as an act of vengeance. He hoped the Europeans would reconcile and prevent further bloodshed.

The Versailles treaty didn't destroy Germany as Clemenceau hoped. However, it suffered greatly. It lost 13% of its territory, returned Alsace and Lorraine to France, was prohibited from having submarines and an air force, and paid 6.6 billion euros in reparations. They also accepted blame for the war.

The treaty was a victory for the Allies as it secured world peace and protected French borders from any future attacks. However, the German people were outraged and found the terms of the treaty to be unfair. The clause that angered them the most was Germany's acceptance of war guilt.

The German government felt pressured by its people, so they decided to renegotiate the treaty. This led to more issues between Germany and the Allied forces, which eventually seeped into the Second World War.

44. Did Churchill Save Britain?

Sir Winston Churchill holds the distinction of being Britain's only prime minister to have served for a total of ten years in nonconsecutive terms from 1940 to 1945 and again from 1951 to 1955. He gained recognition as one of the greatest political figures globally and continues to be held in high esteem by many.

Churchill assumed office during one of the periods in British history, specifically during the Second World War. His first day as Prime Minister coincided with Germany's invasion of France, Holland, and Belgium. Moreover, he confronted the events at Dunkirk, where his leadership demonstrated his aptitude for the role. By making the decision to mobilize all water vessels, both military and civilian, to rescue Allied troops, Churchill played a pivotal role in saving hundreds of thousands of soldiers and ultimately securing victory against Germany.

The majority of citizens showed unwavering support for Churchill. They had complete faith in his ability to lead them towards triumph over Hitler. Renowned for his intellect and astute decision-making skills during times of adversity, he devised political strategies that repeatedly safeguarded Britain's interests. This was most evident during Dunkirk, a moment that put Britain's resilience to its greatest test yet.

With his commanding presence, he forged the *Big Three Alliance* alongside Russia and the United States. Had Britain been led by a different prime minister during the Second World War, Europe's destiny could have taken a very different path.

To answer the question, yes, Sir Winston Churchill saved Britain and even the whole Western civilization. Thanks to his wise leadership, the country managed to stay in the Second World War and achieve victory. He was different from David Lloyd George, who admired Hitler, which might have clouded his judgments at the time. However, Churchill didn't share the same sentiment and was only focused on saving his country.

45. The Blitz and the London Underground

During World War I and II, the British sought refuge in the London Underground to escape the horrors of the raids. The First World War shocked the people as it was the first time they had experienced this kind of brutality in modern history. They found their only refuge was in the tube stations.

In the Second World War, people knew what to expect, but many were reluctant to use the Underground again. However, with the extensive attacks on London, they had no other choice.

On May 31, 1915, London experienced its first airstrike, leading people to hide in the tubes. Living underground was extremely hard, but they had to sacrifice their comfort to survive and keep their families safe.

The English also experienced their first blackout. Indoor lights were concealed, and streetlights were extinguished to prevent the Germans from finding their targets. Even underground lights were turned off, leaving the Londoners anxious and terrified.

As with any war, it was heartbreaking how people gathered in one place, sitting in the dark with their suitcases and crying children holding their teddy bears, hoping all of this would end soon. The English believed that Great Britain would be victorious. They kept their "Keep calm and carry on" spirit. They hung statements like "Bombed but not defeated" and "London can take it" on the underground walls. Their patriotism never wavered, which resulted in the term "the Blitz spirit."

During the war, Germany attacked London 17 times, and 667 people lost their lives. If it wasn't for the London underground, there would have been much more casualties.

These stories show how Great Britain went through many trials and tribulations over the years. Through the wars and struggles, the British also had hope and perseverance for a better day.

Chapter 10: Stories on the Dawn of Modern England

Welcome to the dawn of modern England. It was a long journey to get here, but as you can see from the previous chapters, Britain has a very rich history. And all these aforementioned events have impacted the British world we know today. You may be familiar with some of the stories featured in this chapter. You either have lived through them or heard about them from an older family member.

The Beatles – one of the many British bands that transformed the music scene.[10]

46. The Rise of British Music

Can you even imagine what the world would be like if we didn't have music from bands like The Beatles? Would the music industry be as vibrant without the influence of the Queen? It's impossible to discuss history without acknowledging its profound impact on music.

Back in the 1960s, a new term emerged; "The British Invasion." But this invasion didn't involve Britain conquering nations; rather it was a phenomenon that completely revolutionized the global music scene. It referred to acts, such as The Beatles, Queen, and The Rolling Stones, gaining popularity in the United States and reshaping the entire landscape of music.

In the 1950s, British musicians were captivated by the image projected by rock and roll bands. However, despite their attempts to replicate it, they fell short. Eventually, things changed with the rise of jazz music. Many young people were drawn to its "do it yourself" ethos and found inspiration to start writing their songs.

Bands from all corners of the UK decided to blend British influences to forge their distinctive musical movement. One of the prominent movements in Britain was Merseybeat, which originated in Liverpool. It served as a source of inspiration for artists, including a small band from Liverpool who chose to name themselves "The Beatles."

At the time, British musicians were gaining immense popularity. Many sought to captivate audiences. The first British song to climb the Hot 100 Summit was "Telstar" by The Tornados. Teenagers and young Americans who identified as Mods and Rockers showed great interest in British music.

The British invasion reached its peak with the emergence of The Beatles, considered one of the greatest bands ever. The obsession with The Beatles initially took hold in Britain before spreading. An article published by The Washington Post highlighted how young people in England were going wild over them.

On November 4th, The Beatles performed in front of the Queen Mother, capturing much attention. Their performance had an impact on audiences and the media couldn't get enough of them, gradually forming a cultural phenomenon that became known as "Beatlemania."

Beatlemania quickly spread throughout America; discussions about them dominated news outlets while their songs received airtime on TV and radio stations. Americans fell head over heels for The Beatles, a love that has continued to this day.

There is a captivating tale about a girl who wrote a letter to a radio station after watching The Beatles on TV. She wondered why America didn't have proper music.

On December 17th, the radio station played The Beatles song "I Want to Hold Your Hand." Americans fell head over heels for this song and hurried to record stores to buy it. They even called the radio station requesting it to be played again. Beatlemania had infected the nation. There seemed to be no cure for it. In 1964, "I Want to Hold Your Hand" topped the charts as the number-one song in the country.

Following this, The Beatles made their way to America, leading a news anchor to declare that the British invasion was now known as Beatlemania. Their first appearance on television took place on the Ed Sullivan Show and set TV records that night with nearly half of the US population tuning in.

This was just the beginning of the British Invasion. Numerous other bands, such as The Animals and The Rolling Stones achieved success in America.

Decades have passed since these bands emerged, and their influence remains strong and vibrant today.

Numerous musical groups and individual artists originating from the United Kingdom, such as Adele, Oasis, Blur, and One Direction, have achieved great levels of popularity and triumph in the United States and the world as a whole.

47. The Suffragette Movement

Throughout history, women have faced severe discrimination, being treated as second-class citizens and considered inferior to men. Numerous movements emerged to advocate for equality, one of which was the Suffragette movement.

Emmeline Pankhurst and her daughters. Christabel, Sylvia, and Adela Pankhurst initiated the Suffragette movement in Manchester with the aim of demanding women's right to vote. Their efforts made history when the government granted voting rights to women over 30 years of age, female university graduates, and female property owners. While this was a milestone for women's rights, it was clear that there was still a way to go. In 1903, they established the Women's Social and Political Union

(WSPU) as a means of raising awareness about the Suffragette Movement. The WSPU firmly believed in "actions speaking louder than words."

The Suffragette movement predominantly advocated for rights for women through various means. They tirelessly worked towards their cause for more than a decade. Unfortunately, they fell short of achieving their goals. It was at this point that Emmeline realized that the peaceful approach adopted by her predecessors wasn't yielding the desired results, prompting her to shift strategies.

The women grew weary of relying on their words as nobody seemed to pay attention to them. Instead, they decided to embrace their motto and allow their actions to speak for themselves.

Emmeline and the women in her group used violence to express their demands. They destroyed shop fronts and pillar boxes, and some even bought gun licenses to give the impression that they were ready for a revolution.

They moved WSPU headquarters to London, giving them the chance to protest near the government so they were seen and heard. They protested at Downing Street, heckled members of Parliament, and some went to the extent of chaining themselves to government buildings. Some protesters tried to destroy classic works of art like The Toilette of Venus by François Boucher.

In 1908, the WSPU held a meeting with all its members. Women came from every part of Britain. It was the first time all the members came together. They agreed to march in different parts of the country to protest against voting inequality. 300,000 women took to the streets demanding to be treated as human beings.

Although they had good intentions, their actions weren't acceptable to society, and they were arrested and thrown in prison. They were tortured and treated horribly. The women went on a hunger strike in protest. However, this made the situation worse. The woman who got weak or ill because of the hunger strike was allowed to leave prison with a permit. Once they regained their health and felt better, the police would arrest them again and return them to prison.

However, if they protested or joined the Suffragette movement, they would return to prison, even if they hadn't recovered! This new law was called "The Cat and Mouse Act."

During World War I, the government banned any type of protest. The Suffragettes spent their time supporting the troops. The women were also released from prison during this time, putting an end to the hunger strikes.

Even though the Suffragette women did everything in their power, they couldn't achieve the vote. However, this paved the way for many other women to speak up and take active roles in society.

The Impact of the Industrial Revolution on Modern Britain

The Industrial Revolution had a huge impact on Modern Britain. It didn't only change the country's economy but also the daily lives of the people. The British people were farmers and lived in rural areas. The Industrial Revolution introduced factories and machines and changed the lives of British people forever. Manual labor like stage coaches businesses and hand-weaving became a thing of the past as people were relying on machines.

The Industrial Revolution also changed the way people commuted. Methods of transportation were revolutionized, with trains and railroads taking off, making life faster and easier. People didn't have to travel for days just to visit their families in another city. They just got on a train and reached their destination in a couple of hours. People felt connected and close to each other as everyone they knew was just a ride away.

People were able to afford many products and goods as the economy was booming, and there were many job opportunities. New factories were built every day, providing jobs for people from all walks of life. However, nothing is free. Britain moved away from the clean and quiet rural life into the loud, crowded, and polluted industrial cities. Crime increased, and life became more dangerous than it used to be.

Life was faster than ever before. With the invention of new machines, people could make whatever they wanted in minutes rather than hours. For instance, in Prehistoric England, they used to sew using animal bones; then they discovered threads and needles. In the Industrial Age, they used sewing machines so they could make clothes in days rather than weeks.

Britain was changing rapidly. It was no longer a simple agricultural country. Thanks to the Industrial Revolution, they were able to build viaducts, bridges, and buildings. Britain became a developed country, a far cry from what it was like during the Prehistoric era and Viking age.

Farmers also reaped the benefits of the revolution. It was an era of innovation, with the invention and manufacturing of tools that farmers relied on to cultivate their lands and simplify their lives.

Moreover, the industries of steel, iron and coal thrived during this age. These resources served as fuel for machines and were essential for factories to operate effectively.

As factories sprouted in cities, urban life experienced a boost. The city's population swelled while villages and small towns saw a decline. People flocked to reside near these factories due to the job opportunities they offered – both men and women, even children, found themselves in demand.

The advent of transportation methods further enticed people to settle in cities where accessibility was paramount. Although trains were a novice invention, they became an important means of travel for people from various social classes.

The Industrial Revolution showcased Britain's flourishing state to the world and subsequently spurred its spread across other European nations. This revolution played a role in boosting Britain's population from 6 million people to 21 million during the century. Cities like Halifax, Sheffield, Liverpool, and Manchester became some of the most densely populated areas in the country.

In this shift, the British population experienced a disinterest in rural living and instead opted to relocate to urban areas.

Although living in the city provided them with great opportunities, it had its disadvantages. The factories increased pollution levels in the air. They also were poorly sanitized, making people ill and contributing to the spread of various diseases.

Another disadvantage to the Industrial Revolution was child labor. There weren't any laws protecting children, and they had to work under tough conditions. Poor parents preferred their children to work in the factories rather than go to school as they needed extra income.

Like anything in the world, the industrial era had its advantages and disadvantages. There is no denying that it was a big part of Britain's history, and its impact is still felt to this day.

48. The Swinging Sixties

The era known as the Swinging Sixties occurred between 1964 and 1970, leaving a lasting impact on history by transforming British culture and society. Without a doubt, Britain would have looked remarkably different if it hadn't been for the influence of this period.

During those years, Harold Wilson served as Britain's Prime Minister and supported the shifting dynamics and scientific advancements taking place in the country. Wilson cleverly appealed to the public's desire for progress, promising to propel the nation if they voted for him. Recognizing that people were primarily focused on innovation and growth, this promise secured his victory.

The 1960s witnessed changes in society, culture, and values. A spirit of rebellion swept through the people who found themselves leading different lives from their parent's generation and grappling with finding common ground. These teenagers grew up amidst prosperity while their parents endured the hardships of the Great Depression. Given their circumstances, they had the freedom to simply be themselves – enjoying their youth, having fun, or pushing against societal norms.

This new generation was well-educated and understood that they shouldn't blindly adhere to outdated traditions or conventions. They began questioning established norms and beliefs while also having time, resources, and liberty to explore ideas in order to discover their own identities and aspirations.

During the 1960's, there were styles that appealed to people. Some embraced the Mod style, opting for fashionable attire while riding scooters. On the other hand, there were those who identified as rockers, donning leather jackets and riding motorcycles. Mods and rockers often displayed anger, rebelliousness, and antisocial behavior.

Teenagers and young individuals in that era were greatly influenced by radio, magazines, and TV shows. As they embarked on a journey of self-discovery, the media capitalized on their confusion by featuring The Beatles or slim models on magazine covers, creating a perception that they should emulate their appearance and style. This is somewhat similar to the way social media currently promotes airbrushed photos and sets beauty standards.

Despite experiencing freedom and financial stability during the 1960's in Britain, certain groups (such as women) still faced struggles with inequality. Feminism was an emerging movement at that time, with many taking to the streets to demand rights like legalized abortion. Moreover, thousands of individuals protested against Britain's involvement in the Vietnam War outside of the US Embassy. These protests turned aggressive at times, resulting in riots and hundreds of arrests.

49. Queen Elizabeth II

One can't talk about Britain's modern history without mentioning the woman who shaped it, Queen Elizabeth II. Queen Elizabeth II's reign lasted for a little over 70 years, making her the longest-reigning British monarch. Interestingly, Elizabeth wasn't supposed to be a queen. She was the third in line to the throne after her uncle and father. She wasn't raised to be a queen but to lead a normal life, or as normal as it could be for the king's niece.

Her uncle Edward was the King of England, but he fell in love with a divorced American woman called Wallis Simpson and wanted to marry her. Marrying a divorcee wasn't allowed, so he chose to follow his heart and abdicated the throne. His brother Albert, Elizabeth's father, became the new King of England. She was 10 at the time, and her life turned upside down as she had to be prepared for her new role.

She married her first love, Royal Navy officer Philip Mountbatten, when she was 21 and had four children with him. She gave birth to Charles and Anne before she became queen – and Andrew and Edward afterward.

When Elizabeth was 26 years old, she was on a trip to Kenya with her husband. There, she received news that turned her world upside down. Her father had passed away, and she was the Queen of England. She was very young at the time, and this wasn't an easy responsibility. However, she vowed to the people of Britain to spend her life serving them and the country.

Whether a person is a royalist or not, no one can deny that Queen Elizabeth II was one of the most significant figures in modern English history. She only cared about her country and the royal family. She always presented a united front even when scandals of members of the royal family were headlines in the papers, like Prince Charles and Princess Diana's divorce or the feud between her grandsons, Prince William and Prince Harry.

In her 70 years of leadership, the Queen achieved so much for the country and monarchy. She modernized the royal family by giving its female members the same rights as the males. She also supported thousands of charities in Britain and other countries around the world. She was the first monarch in 100 years to visit Ireland. The historic visit strengthened the relationship between the two countries and was a message of love and peace.

She was loved and highly respected by her people. This was evident after her death, with the whole nation mourning her, and why wouldn't they? Queen Elizabeth II served her country well with class, dignity, and strength. Even when the royal family faced their toughest tests, she always met the public with a smile and followed the family's motto of never complaining, never explaining.

Britain's modern history is as rich as its ancient history. The country has influenced the whole world in every aspect. Whether it was the Industrial Revolution, classical literature, or music, all eyes have always been on Britain.

Conclusion

Throughout history, we can learn many lessons by studying the experiences of those who came before us. Britain, as an empire, has a captivating history filled with intriguing stories, controversies, and significant events that shaped the course of time.

This book delves into each era of history, starting with Prehistoric England. It takes readers on an enthralling journey to one of the country's landmarks, Stonehenge. The book explores theories surrounding its construction and purpose while providing insights into the lives of people during those times.

Continuing the adventure, the book then transports readers to the era of Vikings. Beyond folklore and mythology, it uncovers events that had an impact on Britain's fate, offering captivating stories about how these invaders shaped its destiny.

Among the most important moments in British history lies the Norman Conquest. Following King Edwards passing, Britain underwent a tremendous transformation. The battles for power and the rise and fall of rulers make it reminiscent of a tale from Game of Thrones.

History is replete with royals, unlikable more than likable ones. However, these are often the ones that cause a stir and incite people to reshape history. The book provides an account of King John's nature and how the people rebelled against him and removed him from power. This narrative illustrates the strength of action and how it can bring about change.

Moving on, we delve into the Hundred Years War, an era brimming with tales of conflict featuring prominent figures such as Joan of Arc.

The book also transports you to two captivating figures from history; King Henry and Anne Boleyn. You may be familiar with their love story as it has been portrayed in numerous films and television shows. King Henry was deeply enamored with Anne to the point that he altered his country's laws for her. However, he also made the decision to have her executed, a choice that haunted him for the remainder of his life.

England has always been celebrated for its minds and literary luminaries. The stories surrounding the Age of Enlightenment demonstrate how Britain transitioned from the Dark Ages to embracing advancements while fostering a culture steeped in literature. Witnessing their transformation from an existence during times to becoming one of the world's most cultured nations is undeniably fascinating.

The story of the rise of the British Empire is truly fascinating. Often surrounded by controversy, especially when considering its evolution over the centuries. In this part of the book, the initial section narrates the experiences of soldiers during both World Wars and their immense struggles to safeguard their nation. These stories offer lessons emphasizing the importance of maintaining hope in dire circumstances. The final chapter explores moments such as The Beatles' impact on the music scene.

Throughout Britain's history, from ancient times to today, every event has played a crucial role in shaping its society, culture, and politics. Just imagine how different England would be today if King Henry hadn't separated the state from the church. Similarly, consider what might have happened in Europe if no one had come to rescue soldiers at Dunkirk!

We hope that by deep-diving into English history throughout this book, you have gained an understanding and appreciation for its characters and compelling events.

If you enjoyed this book, a review on Amazon would be greatly appreciated because it would mean a lot to hear from you.

To leave a review:

1. Open your camera app.
2. Point your mobile device at the QR code.
3. The review page will appear in your web browser.

Thanks for your support!

Check out another book in the series

Welcome Aboard, Check Out This Limited-Time Free Bonus!

Ahoy, reader! Welcome to the Ahoy Publications family, and thanks for snagging a copy of this book! Since you've chosen to join us on this journey, we'd like to offer you something special.

Check out the link below for a FREE e-book filled with delightful facts about American History.

But that's not all - you'll also have access to our exclusive email list with even more free e-books and insider knowledge. Well, what are ye waiting for? Click the link below to join and set sail toward exciting adventures in American History.

Access your bonus here

https://ahoypublications.com/

Or, Scan the QR code!

References

(N.d.). Org. uk. https://www.historic-cornwall.org.uk/the-power-of-stonehenge-a-pagan-perspective/#:~:text=For%20many%20pagans%2C%20Stonehenge%20is,to%20seek%20guidance%20and%20clarity.

(N.d.). Parliament.uk. https://www.parliament.uk/about/living-heritage/evolutionofparliament/originsofparliament/birthofparliament/overview/magnacarta/

(N.d.). Royal.uk. https://www.royal.uk/alfred-great-r-871-899

(N.d.). Royal.uk. https://www.royal.uk/henry-viii

(N.d.). Yourstory.com. https://yourstory.com/2023/05/operation-dynamo-dunkirk-evacuation-world-war-2-may-26

An introduction to prehistoric England. (n.d.). English Heritage. https://www.english-heritage.org.uk/learn/story-of-england/prehistory/

Asia Pacific Foundation of Canada. (2017). The Opium Wars in China. Asia Pacific Curriculum. https://asiapacificcurriculum.ca/learning-module/opium-wars-china#:~:text=The%20Opium%20Wars%20in%20the,China%20lost%20both%20wars.

AstroPages. (n.d.). Wwu.edu. https://www.wwu.edu/astro101/stonehenge.shtml

Barrett, C. (2018, April 6). Hundred years' war: Joan of arc and the siege of Orléans. HistoryNet. https://www.historynet.com/hundred-years-war-joan-arc-siege-orleans/

Battle of Agincourt. (2010, July 21). HISTORY. https://www.history.com/this-day-in-history/battle-of-agincourt

Beyer, G. (2023, April 14). Ragnar Lodbrok and his viking family. TheCollector. https://www.thecollector.com/ragnar-lodbrok-and-family/

Beyer, G. (2023, July 30). Battle of the Somme: A sunlit picture of hell. TheCollector. https://www.thecollector.com/battle-of-somme/

Boddy-Evans, A. (2019). Events leading to the Scramble for Africa. ThoughtCo. https://www.thoughtco.com/what-caused-the-scramble-for-africa-43730

Britain Express. (n.d.). Bronze Age England and Wales, the beaker people. Britain Express. https://www.britainexpress.com/History/Bronze_Age.htm

BRITAIN-The official magazine. (2015, June 23). Henry VIII: King of England. Britain Magazine | The Official Magazine of Visit Britain | Best of British History, Royal Family, Travel and Culture. https://britain-magazine.telegraph.co.uk/features/the-two-sides-of-henry-viii/

British Library. (n.d.). Www.bl.uk. https://www.bl.uk/people/william-the-conqueror

British Library. (n.d.-a). Www.bl.uk. https://www.bl.uk/magna-carta

British Library. (n.d.-b). Www.bl.uk. https://www.bl.uk/magna-carta/articles/magna-carta-an-introduction

British Library. (n.d.-c). Www.bl.uk. https://www.bl.uk/magna-carta/videos/what-is-magna-carta

Cartwright, M. (2019). The impact of the Norman conquest of England. World History Encyclopedia. https://www.worldhistory.org/article/1323/the-impact-of-the-norman-conquest-of-england/

Cartwright, M. (2020a). Battle of Agincourt. World History Encyclopedia. https://www.worldhistory.org/Battle_of_Agincourt/

Cartwright, M. (2020b). Edward the Black Prince. World History Encyclopedia. https://www.worldhistory.org/Edward_the_Black_Prince/

Cartwright, M. (2020c). Hundred Years' War. World History Encyclopedia. https://www.worldhistory.org/Hundred_Years'_War/

Cartwright, M. (2023). The impact of the British Industrial Revolution. World History Encyclopedia. https://www.worldhistory.org/article/2226/the-impact-of-the-british-industrial-revolution/

Cavendish, R. (n.d.). End of the Hundred Years War. Historytoday.com. https://www.historytoday.com/archive/end-hundred-years-war

Cohen, J. (2010, December 14). Solving the riddle of Stonehenge's construction. HISTORY. https://www.history.com/news/solving-the-riddle-of-stonehenges-construction

Edward The Black Prince. (2019, November 8). Historic UK.
https://www.historic-uk.com/HistoryUK/HistoryofEngland/Edward-The-Black-Prince/

Enlightenment Thinkers. (n.d.). StudySmarter UK.
https://www.studysmarter.co.uk/explanations/history/european-history/enlightenment-thinkers/

Enstam, G. (2017, November 7). "The Scottish Enlightenment and Literary Culture" edited by Ralph McLean, Ronnie Young, and Kenneth Simpson. The Bottle Imp. https://www.thebottleimp.org.uk/2017/11/scottish-enlightenment-literary-culture-edited-ralph-mclean-ronnie-young-kenneth-simpson/

Forbes, S. (2014, September 30). The man who saved Western civilization -- and how he did it. Forbes.
https://www.forbes.com/sites/steveforbes/2014/09/30/what-we-owe-churchill/?sh=21f19bd6e71f

Galvez, C. (2022, September 8). Remembering Queen Elizabeth II and her achievements. Toast Life; Toast Media Inc.
https://mytoastlife.com/remembering-queen-elizabeth-ii-and-her-achievements/

Henry VIII - Reformation, Divorce, Monarchy. (n.d.). In Encyclopedia Britannica.

Henry VIII wives: facts for kids. (2023, May 3). National Geographic Kids.
https://www.natgeokids.com/uk/discover/history/monarchy/wives-of-henry-viii/

Henry VIII. (2016, October 9). Historic UK. https://www.historic-uk.com/HistoryUK/HistoryofEngland/Henry-VIII/

Henry VIII. (n.d.). Historic Royal Palaces. https://www.hrp.org.uk/hampton-court-palace/history-and-stories/henry-viii/

History Hit. (n.d.). Why did the Vikings invade Britain? History Hit.
https://www.historyhit.com/why-did-the-vikings-invade-britain/

How Churchill led Britain to victory in the Second World War. (n.d.).
Imperial War Museums. https://www.iwm.org.uk/history/how-churchill-led-britain-to-victory-in-the-second-world-war

How long did Queen Elizabeth last as Queen? - Google Search. (n.d.).
Google.com.
https://www.google.com/search?sca_esv=565412338&sxsrf=AM9HkKkEvo_Vx6s20uBZ5exVcEJKv0_x5Q:1694740978816&q=How+long+did+Queen+Elizabeth+last+as+Queen%3F&sa=X&ved=2ahUKEwj67ZyQuquBAxW0XaQEHQBHAYAQzmd6BAgiEAY

How many children did Henry VIII have? (n.d.). Rmg.co.uk.
https://www.rmg.co.uk/stories/topics/how-many-children-did-henry-viii-have

Hundred Years' War - From the Treaty of Brétigny to the accession of Henry V (1360–1413). (n.d.). In Encyclopedia Britannica.

Hundred Years' War - Significance of the Hundred Years' War. (n.d.). In Encyclopedia Britannica.

Introductory Astronomy: Stonehenge. (n.d.). Wsu.edu. http://astro.wsu.edu/worthey/astro/html/im-lab/stonehenge/stonehenge.html

Janssen, V. (2018, October 29). WWI's Christmas truce: When fighting paused for the holiday. HISTORY. https://www.history.com/news/christmas-truce-1914-world-war-i-soldier-accounts

Jarus, O. (2020, March 11). Lindisfarne: The "Holy Island" where Vikings spilled the "blood of saints." Livescience.com; Live Science. https://www.livescience.com/lindisfarne.html

Jarus, O. (2022, September 27). Did druids build Stonehenge? Live Science. https://www.livescience.com/did-druids-build-stonehenge

Jarus, O. (2023, March 21). Where is Stonehenge, who built the prehistoric monument, and how? Livescience.com; Live Science. https://www.livescience.com/stonehenge-england-ancient-history

Joan of Arc. (2009, November 9). HISTORY. https://www.history.com/topics/middle-ages/saint-joan-of-arc

Kaplan, A. (2022, September 9). Elizabeth wasn't originally raised to be queen. How she became Britain's longest-reigning monarch. TODAY. https://www.today.com/news/news/elizabeth-wasnt-originally-raised-queen-became-britains-longest-reigni-rcna46982

Lochun, K. (2020, May 6). Alfred the Great and Edington: how the King of Wessex became great. HistoryExtra. https://www.historyextra.com/period/anglo-saxon/king-alfred-why-great-battle-edington-somerset-marshes-burn-cakes/

Mackenzie, L. (n.d.). What was the significance of the Viking attack on Lindisfarne? History Hit. https://www.historyhit.com/what-was-the-significance-of-the-viking-attack-on-lindisfarne/

Magna Carta summary (1215), Petition of Right - human rights. (n.d.). United for Human Rights. https://www.humanrights.com/what-are-human-rights/brief-history/magna-carta.html

Magna Carta. (2015, October 6). National Archives. https://www.archives.gov/exhibits/featured-documents/magna-carta

Marco, S. (2021, October 30). Beaker people and Stonehenge. Odysseytraveller.com; Odyssey Traveller. https://www.odysseytraveller.com/articles/bronze-age-beaker-people-of-stonehenge/

Marsh, A. (2022, June 21). In 793AD, Vikings attacked Lindisfarne. Here's why it was so shocking. National Geographic.

https://www.nationalgeographic.co.uk/history-and-civilisation/2022/06/in-793ad-vikings-attacked-lindisfarne-heres-why-it-was-so-shocking

Martinez, J. (2022). Battle of Agincourt. In Encyclopedia Britannica.

McCrum, R. (2015, September 26). Agincourt was a battle like no other … but how do the French remember it? The Guardian. https://www.theguardian.com/world/2015/sep/26/agincourt-600th-anniversary-how-french-remember-it

McLean, A. P. J. (n.d.). The hundred years' war. Lumenlearning.com. https://courses.lumenlearning.com/atd-herkimer-westerncivilization/chapter/the-hundred-years-war/

Military History Monthly. (2022, January 12). Edward III, the black prince, and the battle of crécy. The Past. https://the-past.com/feature/edward-iii-the-black-prince-and-the-battle-of-crecy/

Museum of London. (2021, July 27). Who were the Suffragettes? Museum of London. https://www.museumoflondon.org.uk/museum-london/explore/who-were-suffragettes

Nadeau, S. (2016, December 24). How did the 1914 WWI Christmas Truce happen? Solosophie. https://www.solosophie.com/wwi-propaganda-and-christmas-truce-1914/

Nikel, D. (2022, October 22). Danelaw explained: When the Vikings ruled in England. Life in Norway. https://www.lifeinnorway.net/danelaw-explained/

No title. (n.d.-a). Study.com. https://study.com/academy/lesson/the-100-years-war-england-vs-france.html

No title. (n.d.-b). Study.com. https://study.com/academy/lesson/joan-of-arc-and-the-end-of-the-100-years-war.html

Norman conquest. (n.d.). Nationalgeographic.org. https://education.nationalgeographic.org/resource/norman-conquest/

Owens, J. (2017, January 21). Stonehenge. National Geographic. https://www.nationalgeographic.com/history/article/stonehenge-1

Paese, M. (n.d.). British invasion. Thehistoryofrockandroll.net. https://thehistoryofrockandroll.net/british-invasion/

Plesz, O. (2017, March 17). Joan of Arc and the hundred-year war. Manchester Historian. https://manchesterhistorian.com/2017/joan-of-arc-and-the-hundred-years-war/

Porter, G. (2021, February 10). The holy island of Lindisfarne - the Viking attack. Org.uk. https://www.lindisfarne.org.uk/793/

Prehistoric Britain. (2015, March 28). Historic UK. https://www.historic-uk.com/HistoryUK/HistoryofEngland/Prehistoric-Britain/

Prehistory: Daily life. (n.d.). English Heritage. https://www.english-heritage.org.uk/learn/story-of-england/prehistory/daily-life/

Ragnar Lothbrok: the legend of the immortal Viking and his sons. (2019, December 6). HistoryExtra. https://www.historyextra.com/period/viking/ragnar-lothbrok-the-immortal-viking/

Rebellions against William. (n.d.). Gcsehistory.com. https://www.gcsehistory.com/faq/rebellions.html

Royal Collection Trust. (2009, November 9). Henry VIII. HISTORY. https://www.history.com/topics/european-history/henry-viii

Shaw, I. P. (2023). Edward The Black Prince. In Encyclopedia Britannica.

Short, E. (2023, January 29). Dunkirk and the real story of the World War II military disaster. MovieWeb. https://movieweb.com/dunkirk-true-story-ww2/

Shuttleworth, M. (n.d.). Neolithic astronomy. Explorable.com. https://explorable.com/neolithic-astronomy

Sir Winston Churchill. (n.d.). Gov.uk. https://www.gov.uk/government/history/past-prime-ministers/winston-churchill

Sky HISTORY. (n.d.). The Three Greatest Viking Battles. Sky HISTORY TV Channel. https://www.history.co.uk/shows/the-real-vikings/articles/the-three-greatest-viking-battles

St. Joan of Arc - French Heroine, Martyr, Trial. (n.d.). In Encyclopedia Britannica.

Stonehenge. (2010, June 1). HISTORY. https://www.history.com/topics/european-history/stonehenge

Swinging sixties: Definition, Culture & Meaning. (n.d.). StudySmarter UK. https://www.studysmarter.co.uk/explanations/history/modern-britain/the-swinging-sixties/

The Battle of Hastings. (2016, April 18). Historic UK. https://www.historic-uk.com/HistoryMagazine/DestinationsUK/The-Battle-of-Hastings/

The battle of Stamford Bridge. (2021, August 30). Historic UK. https://www.historic-uk.com/HistoryMagazine/DestinationsUK/The-Battle-of-Stamford-Bridge/

The Editors of Encyclopaedia Britannica. (2023, September 10). East India Company | Definition, History, & Facts. Encyclopedia Britannica. https://www.britannica.com/money/topic/East-India-Company

The Editors of Encyclopedia Britannica. (2022). The Enlightenment Causes and Effects. In Encyclopedia Britannica.

The Editors of Encyclopedia Britannica. (2023). Druid. In Encyclopedia Britannica.

The Editors of Encyclopedia Britannica. (2023). Ragnar Lothbrok. In Encyclopedia Britannica.

The Enlightenment: Adam Smith: 1723 – 1790. (n.d.). Saylor Academy. https://learn.saylor.org/mod/book/view.php?id=54704&chapterid=40124

The five boroughs of Danelaw. (2019, July 25). Historic UK. https://www.historic-uk.com/HistoryUK/HistoryofEngland/The-Five-Boroughs-Of-Danelaw/

The Great Heathen Army of Vikings that invaded England. (2021, April 12). HeritageDaily - Archaeology News. https://www.heritagedaily.com/2021/04/the-great-heathen-army-of-vikings-that-invaded-england/138660

The great heathen army. (2019, March 20). Historic UK. https://www.historic-uk.com/HistoryUK/HistoryofEngland/Great-Heathen-Army/

The history of the Magna Carta. (2019, May 31). Historic UK. https://www.historic-uk.com/HistoryUK/HistoryofEngland/The-Origins-of-the-Magna-Carta/

The history of the Vikings in England. (n.d.). English Heritage. https://www.english-heritage.org.uk/visit/inspire-me/the-history-of-vikings-in-england/

The history press. (n.d.). Thehistorypress.co.uk. https://www.thehistorypress.co.uk/women-s-history/suffragettes/

The Importance of the Eclipse in Ancient Society. (n.d.). Encyclopedia.com. https://www.encyclopedia.com/science/encyclopedias-almanacs-transcripts-and-maps/importance-eclipse-ancient-society

The National Archives. (n.d.). The national archives - homepage. https://www.nationalarchives.gov.uk/education/resources/magna-carta/british-library-magna-carta-1215-runnymede/

The Norman conquest. (2017, September 30). Historic UK. https://www.historic-uk.com/HistoryUK/HistoryofEngland/The-Norman-Conquest/

The origins of the Hundred Years War. (2021, August 31). Historic UK. https://www.historic-uk.com/HistoryUK/HistoryofEngland/Origins-Hundred-Years-War/

The real Ragnar Lothbrok. (2018, November 13). Historic UK. https://www.historic-uk.com/HistoryUK/HistoryofEngland/Ragnar-Lothbrok/

The Scientific Revolution. (2020, April 20). Historic UK. https://www.historic-uk.com/HistoryUK/HistoryofBritain/The-Scientific-Revolution/

The Scramble for Africa | St John's College, University of Cambridge. (n.d.). https://www.joh.cam.ac.uk/library/library_exhibitions/schoolresources/exploration/scramble_for_africa

The Viking Raid on Lindisfarne. (n.d.). English Heritage. https://www.english-heritage.org.uk/visit/places/lindisfarne-priory/History/viking-raid/

The Vikings in Britain: a brief history. (2011, January 13). The Historical Association. https://www.history.org.uk/primary/resource/3867/the-vikings-in-britain-a-brief-history

Théry, J. (2017, April 13). How Joan of Arc turned the tide in the hundred-year war. National Geographic. https://www.nationalgeographic.com/history/history-magazine/article/joan-of-arc-warrior-heretic-saint-martyr

Treaty of Versailles centennial: British aims in Paris. (n.d.). Peacepalacelibrary.Nl. https://peacepalacelibrary.nl/blog/2019/treaty-versailles-centennial-british-aims-paris

Treaty of Versailles. (n.d.). Sky HISTORY TV Channel. https://www.history.co.uk/history-of-ww2/treaty-of-versailles

TVH. (2023, July 30). What was the North Sea Empire?

Understanding Stonehenge. (n.d.). English Heritage. https://www.english-heritage.org.uk/visit/places/stonehenge/history-and-stories/understanding-stonehenge/

Waxman, O. B. (2017, July 20). What to know about the miraculous true story behind Dunkirk. Time. https://time.com/4865358/dunkirk-history-christopher-nolan-film/

Welford, J. (2022, August 22). The end of the Hundred Years War. Medium. https://medium.com/@johnwelford15/the-end-of-the-hundred-years-war-1a315c73c91b

What Is the Enlightenment and How Did It Transform Politics? (n.d.). World101 from the Council on Foreign Relations. https://world101.cfr.org/contemporary-history/prelude-global-era/what-enlightenment-and-how-did-it-transform-politics

What was the "Scramble for Africa"? (n.d.). History Skills. https://www.historyskills.com/classroom/modern-history/scramble-for-africa/

When the Vikings ruled in Britain: A brief history of Danelaw. (n.d.). Sky HISTORY TV Channel. https://www.history.co.uk/articles/when-the-vikings-ruled-in-britain-a-brief-history-of-danelaw

Why did Henry VIII break with Rome? (n.d.). Rmg.co.uk. https://www.rmg.co.uk/stories/topics/why-did-henry-viii-break-rome

Why did the Vikings raid? (2021, March 26). BBC. https://www.bbc.co.uk/bitesize/topics/z939mp3/articles/z7jd8xs

Why the Enlightenment still matters today. (n.d.). Gresham College. https://www.gresham.ac.uk/watch-now/why-enlightenment-still-matters-today

Why was Stonehenge built? (2013, April 10). HISTORY.
https://www.history.com/news/why-was-stonehenge-built

Wilde, R. (2009, December 5). Effects of the Hundred Years War.
ThoughtCo. https://www.thoughtco.com/aftermath-of-the-hundred-years-war-1221904

William I - Norman Conquest, England, Normandy. (n.d.). In Encyclopedia
Britannica.

Wong, D. (2023, April 25). What if Africa was Never Colonized? - Dwayne
Wong (Omowale) - Medium. Medium. https://dwomowale.medium.com/what-if-africa-was-never-colonized-cd480ecb5390#:~:text=Had%20Africa%20not%20been%20colonized,ability%20to%20effectively%20develop%20itself.

Shelter in wartime. (n.d.). London Transport Museum.
https://www.ltmuseum.co.uk/collections/stories/war/shelter-wartime

The blitz spirit. (2018, October 6). Historic UK. https://www.historic-uk.com/HistoryUK/HistoryofBritain/Blitz-Spirit

Image Sources

[1] _https://pixabay.com/photos/sunrise-stonehenge-mystical-england-3901312/_

[2] _https://pixabay.com/photos/ai-generated-man-helmet-7718746/_

[3] _https://pixabay.com/photos/horse-soldier-warrior-war-battle-4596827/_

[4] _https://pixabay.com/photos/england-king-artus-royal-3431451/_

[5] _https://pixabay.com/photos/art-sculpture-medieval-knight-6598445/_

[6] _https://pixabay.com/photos/hans-holbeing-king-henry-viii-91067/_

[7] _https://pixabay.com/photos/adam-smith-edinburgh-statue-4637193/_

[8] _https://pixabay.com/photos/map-map-of-africa-world-map-globe-7299481/_

[9] _https://pixabay.com/photos/soldiers-grave-dig-war-buried-67510/_

[10] _https://pixabay.com/photos/beatles-statue-lennon-mccartney-4612416/_

www.ingramcontent.com/pod-product-compliance
Lightning Source LLC
Chambersburg PA
CBHW071524120626
46550CB00006B/2349